SOUTH BEACH

AMERICA'S RIVIERA, MIAMI BEACH, FLORIDA

PHOTOGRAPHY / WRITING / DESIGN

BY

BILL WISSER

Design Associate — Tom Korba — South Beach Grafix

ARCADE PUBLISHING • NEW YORK

To all my Parents

First Edition

Library of Congress Cataloging-in-Publication Data

Wisser, Bill.
  South Beach : America's Riviera, Miami Beach, Florida / Bill Wisser. — 1st ed.
    p. cm.
  ISBN 1-55970-268-0
  1. South Beach (Miami Beach, Fla.) — Pictorial works. 2. South Beach (Miami Beach, Fla.) — Description and travel. 3. Architecture — Florida, Miami Beach — Pictorial works. 4. Miami Beach (Fla.) — Pictorial works. 5. Miami Beach (Fla.) — Description and travel.
  I. Title.
  F319.M62W57   1994
  975.9´381 — dc20   94-17561

Published in the United States by Arcade Publishing, Inc., New York
Distributed by Little, Brown and Company

10 9 8 7 6 5 4 3 2 1

KPT

Printed in the United States of America

CONTENTS

Cover: **The streamlined Marlin Hotel, designed in 1939 by Tropical Deco master L. Murray Dixon and beautifully renovated by Island Records, movie, and TV mogul Chris Blackwell, who maintains a recording studio and an apartment there, as well as hotel suites and a stunning restaurant and bar.**

Page 1: **South Beach style — Sunday in the park with a tanned young body; a big live snake; and, of course, that essential fashion-biz accessory, the beeper.**

Pages 2 and 3: **The Warsaw. At the corner of Espanola Way and Collins Avenue, this streamlined fantasy of a building was originally Hoffman's Cafeteria, designed by architect Henry Hohauser in 1939, but reincarnated a half-century later as one of South Beach's most torrid discos.**

Page 4: **Lounging on the Deco wall around the swimming pool of the Helen Mar Apartments, designed by Robert E. Collins in 1936, is a cat.**

DECO, SEXY, AN

Above: **Ocean Drive.** *Above right:* **In a Washington Avenue boutique, a mural by Miguel Delgado.** *Below right:* **Go-go**

D CHIC

boys in gaucho gear at a South Beach cabaret.

Mambo, flamenco, reggae, and Brazilian jazz, music from many places is blowing like a warm tropical breeze through the sidewalk cafés on Ocean Drive and over the park toward sunbathers lounging on this celebrated American neighborhood's topless beach. At the bistros, ponytailed businessmen murmur into their cellular phones. In studios, artists work. And on the street, photographers and models do their dance; luscious ladies lunch in gourmet style; tattooed bikers wheel growling Harleys to the curb; tourists from all over wander delighted; while scantily clad, world-famous supermodels and unknown beauties alike sashay down the sunlit sidewalks as if they were fashion show runways.

But from above, from a small seaplane gliding

through warm sunshine on its approach to a white splashdown on blue-green Biscayne Bay, you can see the whole island — a seven-mile-long sandbar, really — lolling in the big bay, with the skyscrapers of downtown Miami jutting like a mountain range in the background.

A tropical jungle once covered the sandbar, but now you see a bustling beach city. And on its Atlantic side is the wide beach, now almost completely fringed with high-rises, except toward the island's southern tip, the part called South Beach.

Suddenly the shoreline is fringed not merely by a beach but also by a great, green park studded with towering palms and, beyond that, crowded boulevards where the buildings are nearly all low-rise, lustrous Art Deco gems, eye-catching anachronisms with tropical touches such as verandas and ceiling fans, plus the futuristic fins and languid curves of what was the modernism of a long-ago era.

Most of South Beach and its Flash Gordon–like fantasy architecture was built during an intense eight-year period, 1934 through 1941. Later, due to ignorance, neglect, and greed, this unique district deteriorated into a fetid slum, a lost city, nearly forgotten and in ruins by the 1970s, when high-rise developers and local politicians, seeing no beauty or profit in the broken-down old neighborhood, tried to demolish it.

Historic preservationists, artists, and unorthodox entrepreneurs fought for two decades to save South Beach — and managed to rescue most of the neighborhood, which was reborn as an international play-ground, artists' colony, and glamour capital for the hip, the rich, and the beautiful — and plenty of other just plain interesting people — who now mix there in a sultry salsa of sex and money, art and commerce, fun and fashion.

Against an American landscape grown increasingly banal, standardized, and automobile-oriented, historic South Beach stands as exhilarating, singular, and pedestrian-friendly. And much to the surprise of the politicians and others who wanted to demolish the neighborhood, it has become a phenomenal real estate success story.

It's not a big place: just one-and-a-half square miles, only a small part of Miami Beach (the fifty-four-square-mile city on the sandbar), which, in turn, is only a small part of a sprawling 2,000-square-mile Miami metro area. Yet tiny South Beach's Tropical Deco dreamscape and old-fashioned pedestrian lifestyle have almost magically helped make this little oceanfront neighborhood big: world-renowned as one of the most beautiful urban places on the planet — and one of its wildest places for partying.

Gorgeous people with beautiful bodies, deep tans, and the bare minimum in clothing whiz by on Rollerblades. They're mostly models or model wannabes attracted to South Beach's pulsating fashion, movie, and club scene.

During the Season (October through March), fashion photo teams, video units, and movie crews from around the world, with all their glittering stars, scurrying stylists, makeup artists, assistants, technicians, lights, cameras, and action, dot South Beach's streets, parks, and beaches with their trucks and trailers, big white scrims and warm gold reflectors. At night, drawn by the beauties, Eurotrash, Arab, Latino, and American playboys (and playgirls) swing their sweet-purring Ferraris, Lamborghinis, and Bentleys up to the well-guarded entrances of South Beach's trendy top restaurants, nightspots, and decadent dives.

Drag queens parade campily through the night, enacting their phantasmagorical role as local omnisex goddesses, mixing with music and movie megastars

Opposite: **The Century Hotel, designed in 1939 by Henry Hohauser and renovated in the '90s, is one of South Beach's most civilized outposts, much favored by the fashion elite. But in the '70s it was one of hundreds of vintage buildings City Hall wanted to demolish.** *Above:* **An American dream on the celebrated sand of South Beach: twenty-one-year-old Yohani is a mortgage broker and a lead singer in a techno-merengué band.**

such as Madonna and Stallone, international socialites, transsexuals, muscle boys, models, dominatrixes, con artists, criminals, social climbers, paparazzi, publicists, and other players, some well known and others totally unsung, from the ultra-

divine, often super-strange demiworlds of music, fashion, art, and sex.

Cavorting with them are hundreds of stylish young club kids and club kittens, many only teenagers. (Even if you're underage, you can get into nearly any South Beach club, no matter how posh, just so long as you look very beautiful, very bizarre, or very creative — or better yet, all three.)

Throw into the party mix hundreds of other scene-makers: famous and not-so-famous artists, art dealers, call girls, call boys, celebutantes (as local gossip columnists call some of the party people), and countless camp followers.

Plus of course tourists, foreign and domestic, including the dreaded "bridge and tunnel people," alien slugs from outlying suburbs who invade in gross numbers on holidays and weekends. Often dismissed as a disastrous tidal wave of fashion undesirables, the supposedly contemptible bridge and tunnel people's eager presence on Friday and Saturday nights probably pays the rent at many a haughty South Beach nightspot. On the other hand, for many hip South Beach habitués who tend to get in for free anyhow, the best and most decadent nights are slightly obscure: Sundays or some late, late nights concealed deep in the middle of the week when most mainlanders with their regular nine-to-five slug lives just can't make it.

And don't forget the high school kids, the news camera crews, the conventioneers, and the groupies. All meld into a gloriously incandescent communal nightlife, at once democratic and exclusive, gay and straight, mindless and stimulating, incredibly boring and hypnotically fascinating.

Meanwhile the painters, fashion designers,

photographers, musicians, writers, dancers, preservationists, entrepreneurs, and other visionaries who helped create the famous South Beach scene (which embraces much more than its Felliniesque nightlife) make the neighborhood's galleries, studios, theaters,

back streets, and offbeat cafés vital.

For behind all the glitter of the scene and the Season, South Beach is a neighborhood: a small town, a place where you know your neighbors. Just a

From left: **Dancer at a club called Paragon; an early morning fashion shoot on Ocean Drive; a stylist preps model Leslie Holecek on an Art Deco rooftop; late-Sunday-night revelry at a restaurant named Bang.** *Overleaf:* **Straight and gay party together in South Beach, from left, actor Stephen Bauer, fashion designer and restaurant owner Debbie Ohanian, and drag queens Adora, Damian Dee-Vine, and Sexcillia, at Debbie's restaurant, Starfish.**

short walk from the neon and frenzy of the nightlife are dozens of quiet, leafy residential streets where many of the scene-makers live. It's like a college town, with plenty of bicycles and young people (though not half so many bookstores or intellectual conversations). Tucked into a metropolis, South Beach is an urban village. On the street, or in food markets, or at the sidewalk cafés, or on the beach, or in the clubs, you're continually bumping into old friends.

South Beach's incredibly dynamic and diverse panorama is unfolding in a tiny, confined neighborhood, yet it often seems like a whole planet: huge, self-referential, and entirely separate from the rest of Miami Beach, not to mention from the rest of the Miami metropolitan area, the rest of the United States, and, indeed, the rest of the known galaxy.

Tiny, alien, Planet South Beach, while different and separate from everywhere else, is not, however, totally isolated; instead, it's a sort of intergalactic

crossroads, a space station where travelers change rocketships. Or, to put it in more down-to-earth terms, South Beach has become the meeting place of three continents: Europe, South America, and North America.

In the '80s and '90s, planeloads of Europeans snapped up South Beach real estate at bargain prices and helped renovate the neighborhood. Wealthy Latin Americans also bought in. South Beach became an international resort, a new Riviera, just as sexy, tropical, and exotic as you can get and still be in the United States. It became commonplace in local discos and cafés to hear Italian, French, German, Dutch, Portuguese, Japanese, Swedish, and, of course, Spanish. From French *Vogue* to American *Playboy*, virtually every fashion and lifestyle magazine in the world was writing ecstatically about sultry South Beach. The town became so cosmopolitan that one joke has it that the great thing about being in South Beach today is that it's almost like being in the United States.

The place was booming. Being on the Beach was almost like being at the edge of a rocketport. Miami's international airport is only fifteen minutes by car from South Beach, and its many flight paths bring airliners flying overhead, perhaps a few thousand feet up. First they turn in slowly over the ocean, and then, starting their descent right above the town's Deco towers, they begin lining up for their approach to the airport nine miles west. Or you can lie on the beach any time (though it's best about an hour before sunset) and watch the silver jets climb gracefully away. The enormous 747s propel themselves majestically, with what almost seems like slowness, into the blueness and out over the Atlantic. At night, older cargo jets with noisier engines roar in from South America, bringing in fresh flowers for all America and who knows what else in their holds. By day, the big white cruise ships — as tall as fifteen-story buildings — plus a myriad of freighters and other vessels, large and small, sail in and out past the southern tip of South Beach, seemingly close enough to touch, in a narrow channel of the busy Port of Miami, further adding to the feeling that you're standing now at the edge of a continent.

With its superb location, warm winter weather, fine restaurants, sizzling nightlife, multilingual culture, and easy connections to Europe, the Caribbean, Latin America, and the United States (particularly the Washington–New York corridor), Miami was, in the last decade of the twentieth century, emerging as a world commercial and communications capital.

The South American, European, and U.S. merchant banks along Brickell Avenue in downtown Miami already constitute Latin America's financial district. In the United States, Miami is second only to New York as an international banking center. Greater Miami is also becoming the communications capital of the Spanish-speaking world.

In 1993 the MTV Latino network began broadcasting by satellite to some twenty-two Spanish-speaking countries from its state-of-the-art studios in a remodeled Art Deco building on South Beach's trendy Lincoln Road. Less than a year later, MTV Latino had become Latin America's most popular cable channel in terms of number of subscribers. This triggered a boom in the production of Spanish-language music videos, many of them shot in the Miami area by new, South Beach–based production companies. Several other major transnational Spanish-language news and entertainment satellite networks were already headquartered in Miami. In addition, Sony Music moved its Latin Music Division into yet another renovated Lincoln Road building.

With all this media based in South Beach or coming through it in caravanlike crews, there are McLuhan moments aplenty in South Beach's little global village. Like, for instance, working out at a local gym in a Deco building and seeing supermodel

Above: **Rocketlike jetliner descends over Planet South Beach's 1947 Delano Hotel, a late Deco masterpiece by architect Robert Swartburg.**
Opposite, above: **For a while South Beach was populated by so many old people that the neighborhood was known as "God's Waiting Room."**
Below: **Felliniesque night moves at the Warsaw.**

Cindy Crawford at the next machine, looking very pretty but not at all superhuman in light makeup, straight hair, and loose-fitting (but bare-midriffed) gray sweats, when suddenly her glamorous, mega-buffed image appears hanging from the ceiling on the gym's TV monitors, which are tuned to MTV and start broadcasting her program, *House of Style*. It is like seeing her in Cindy-rama: she is at the same time three-dimensional and two-dimensional, which seems to add up to five dimensions.

For all its house-of-mirrors glamour and international flavor, South Beach remains down-to-earth American in the same way as New York: a democratic gateway where people can mix, a wide-open city, a world city. But since South Beach is so much smaller than even just the Manhattan part of New York, perhaps it's better to dub South Beach not a great world city, but just a great world village.

Almost all of South Beach's approximately 800 remaining Art Deco buildings — the world's largest concentration of Art Deco structures — have been or are now being renovated into chic hotels, luxury condominiums, townhouses, restaurants, nightclubs, boutiques, offices, and the like. Despite the tragic loss of many beautiful and important South Beach buildings, this mostly private renovation

of nearly an entire neighborhood is one of the greatest historic preservation success stories of the twentieth century.

For strange as it may seem now, only a few years ago South Beach was about as far from prosperous or fashionable as a place can be. It was a broken-down ghetto, a crime-ridden slum in the sun, populated not by supermodels and socialites but by increasingly old, frail, and poverty-stricken Jewish retirees; desperate Third World boat people; warehoused mental patients; and violent hard-core criminals.

The retirees, born, most of them, in Eastern Europe, and now speaking Yiddish or heavily accented English, had come to sunny Florida to live out their last years after working for decades in New York or other big U.S. cities. By the late 1970s and early 1980s other less-than-glamorous groups were also flooding into South Beach, notably thousands of wretchedly poor Cuban immigrants, some of them hardened criminals or mental patients that Castro had kicked out of Cuba.

The lovely Art Deco architecture, built mostly in the 1930s (when South Beach had boomed despite the Depression) had gradually fallen out of fashion and into disrepair during the long, sad period of South Beach's decline, beginning in the 1950s.

By the early '80s, many of what are today's chic hotels and gorgeous little Deco apartment houses were roach-infested crack houses, smelly retirement hotels, government-subsidized group homes for the mentally disturbed, or just pitifully abandoned rotting old hulks.

Greater Miami's business and political elite lacked the vision to see through the slumlike conditions to the beauty underneath. The local establishment wanted only to demolish the old Art Deco neighborhood to make room for glitzy, standard-issue high-rises, shopping centers, and parking lots. The developers and the politicians failed to understand the neighborhood's history — or its future.

In 1995, after South Beach had become a world-renowned attraction, *Miami Herald* architecture critic Beth Dunlop recalled the establishment's attitude during the days of controversy about whether the neighborhood should be saved: "Many people used to tell me, categorically, that the Art Deco District was ugly, that its buildings weren't worth renovating. They're the same people who now lead their out-of-town guests on promenades down Ocean Drive."

The story of South Beach's surprising past, and of the hard-fought battle to save the beautiful but battered buildings and preserve the neighborhood's unique style, will be told in later chapters. But to set the scene, it's good to glance back at the slumlike South Beach of the late 1970s and early 1980s, the low point in its history.

"It was the Dark Ages," remembers Dona Zemo, now a South Beach businesswoman but then one of a tiny band of pioneering Art Deco enthusiasts who had moved to a moribund South Beach and vowed to revive it. The streamlined, music-filled oceanfront verandas where the smart set now meets presented quite a different sight to visitors in the 1970s. Then these elegant verandas were just the dilapidated front porches of crumbling hotels, jammed with tattered aluminum lawn chairs on which the hotels' aging, poor, and often sickly tenants passed their days. Many of the oldsters lived two or three to a hotel room, subsisting on Social Security and Medicare checks.

Back then, Washington Avenue had no boutiques selling $250 vintage collectible Levi jeans to the Euro-rich.

But there were a couple of shabby everything-for-$1 stores stores where you could scrounge for bargains among the cardboard boxes; plenty of

kosher butchers and sweetly aromatic bakeries; plenty of little bodegas where you could buy religious candles with scenes of the Catholic saints stenciled on them and where you could sip super-sweet and strong Cuban coffee in shot-glass-sized paper cups; plenty of slightly flea-bitten but friendly fruit stands where you could buy fresh-squeezed tropical drinks made in an ancient blender under a noisily clanking ceiling fan; plenty of unassuming Cuban barber shops and all-American beauty salons that looked like they had fallen out of the early 1950s in some freakish *Twilight Zone*–like malfunction in time.

Living in this South Beach time warp were funky storefront doctors and cheap dentists, healers, and fortune tellers; numerous synagogues; stooped old ladies with canes and trembling old men with stubbled chins. Burned-out buildings and empty storefronts dotted the streets. So many elderly people in failing health inhabited the place that South Beach was nicknamed "God's Waiting Room."

Walking through the neighborhood "was like being in a nursing home," recalls Patrick Roach, now a hospital technician but then an eleven-year-old boy who came to South Beach to play on a then miserably bleak Lincoln Road. For if South Beach was a nursing home, it was not a luxurious one. "The buildings were literally falling apart, paint was falling off, and the interiors were full of mold," remembers Roach. "Houses were boarded up. Lincoln Road was full of garbage and largely deserted. We'd run through the streets."

In a local theater where he and his friends devoured hot buttered popcorn and cheap second-run movies, the seats were rotting. Roach remembers the rot was so deep that the seats literally stank. This was in the great Lincoln Theater, a once-splendid Art Deco movie palace constructed in 1935. Today, a decade or two after Roach sat in those stinking seats, the Lincoln Theater has been renovated and reborn as

Above: **The Lincoln Theater.** *Opposite:* **Vintage apartment house by Hohauser awaits renovation.**

the handsome concert-hall home of the New World Symphony Orchestra. Unfortunately, much of its Art Deco interior was lost during the decades of decay and then a partial renovation that restored the exterior but stripped the interior.

Lincoln Road, which in the 1930s and 1940s had been the finest shopping street in all Miami, where Saks Fifth Avenue, Bonwit Taylor, Harry Winston Jewelers, and other top stores once reigned, had by the 1980s withered and nearly died. This boulevard, once known as "the Fifth Avenue of the South," was now lined by more than a hundred empty stores.

In 1980 Fidel Castro permitted about 125,000 Cubans to flee to the United States. This great exodus is called the Mariel Boatlift because more than 2,000 boats (many sent by Miami Cubans) plus a numberless flotilla of leaking Cuban rafts concocted from junk — old pieces of wood, inner tubes, Styrofoam packing, and twine — carried desperate escapees across the Straits of Florida in daring voyages to America from a tiny Cuban port, twenty-five miles west of Havana, named Mariel.

Most Cubans who arrived in Miami over the years (including the *Marielitos*, as the 1980 boat people were called) were fine, honest, hard-working people who added brilliantly to Florida's vitality. But during the 159-day Mariel sealift, Castro also set free and exported a large number of his country's undesirables: convicts and mental patients, even a couple of poor, disease-ravaged lepers. An estimated one-fifth of the *Marielitos* had Cuban criminal records — that's about 25,000 criminals. Many were merely anti-Castro political criminals. Others had committed very understandable crimes, such as buying or selling food on the black market. But still others would have been hardcore criminals in any society. Yet all were allowed into the United States because they were fleeing Castro the Communist. And many of these *Marielitos* would add to South Beach's already considerable woes. Castro had dropped what some Americans called "a demographic bomb."

Overwhelmed, Dade County authorities at first channeled the incoming human tidal wave of Cuban boat people into emergency camps set up under the bleachers and in the parking lots of Miami's Orange Bowl football stadium, or in squalid tent cities sprawling beneath portions of the elevated I-95 highway in downtown Miami.

The spectacle of a tropical refugee city festering under the interstate became such a painful public relations eyesore for Miami that the embarrassed authorities eventually resettled many of the new immigrants out of sight, into low-rent rooms in the old-folks' ghetto of South Beach. Many of the boat people were uneducated and poor. Finding jobs was hard. Meanwhile, other penniless Third World immigrants or disadvantaged U.S. groups, such as Americans with mental problems, were also being dumped into South Beach's decaying rooming houses and government-subsidized group homes. Making matters worse, the international cocaine trade began booming, with Miami becoming a major drug capital and trans-shipment point.

What with *Marielitos*, Latin and local drug gangs, and mental patients, South Beach went from a sleepy, if somewhat rundown, retirement town to a "Wild West OK Corral with shootings on Ocean Drive and women being abducted at gunpoint," according to Miami Beach Police Commander Marty Zowarski. Adds Sgt. Andy Caputo, "Nothing used to happen after midnight." But in 1980 that changed: "You'd go all night from call to call: fights, disturbances. A lot of foreign nationals were involved. We needed more troops."

Drug dealing went wild, street crime boomed; killings were commonplace, even on Ocean Drive, South Beach's most important boulevard. Bums and homeless people, many drinking from brown paper bags or doing drugs, clustered on street corners and alleyways, benches and parks. The long-established but more elderly and helpless South Beach residents were finding their neighborhood increasingly dangerous.

Above and opposite: **These two Deco buildings were photographed in the early '90s before they were renovated and turned into condo apartments. The one opposite was designed in 1936 by Hohauser.**

The neighborhood was spiraling downward. Landlords let some old buildings rot. Rotting buildings could command only low rents. But low rents made long-delayed repairs unaffordable. So the rot went deeper. Banks accelerated the decay by redlining the whole neighborhood, refusing loans to anyone who wanted to renovate a building there. City Hall actually forbade renovations south of Sixth Street in an attempt to encourage demolitions. Not every building was in decay, but soon a critical mass of them were. Without proper environmental management, even the beach itself — the very essence of South Beach — was allowed to erode to just a narrow strand.

What had been a stylish and comfortable seaside resort, beginning in the 1920s and lasting through the 1950s, was now in danger of taking a final slide into a pathetic end. Perhaps only "urban renewal" by wrecking ball could put this diseased neighborhood out of its misery.

Today, Manny Hernandez is a paparazzi ace who snaps celebrities in chichi South Beach nightspots for Ron Galella, the New York–based paparazzi king. (Manny is especially remembered in Miami street photography circles for the time he threw himself on Madonna's limo to make it stop.) But back in the early 1980s, Hernandez was just another Cuban-American teenager who came to funky, rundown South Beach on weekends to swim and buy cheap hot dogs. It was dangerous, particularly south of Fifth Street, he recalled years later: "Just walking down there, you could get jumped by the *Marielitos...* [South Beach] buildings, they didn't look like buildings that had been wonderful at one time. No one took care of them...There were just old people in lawn chairs. What you see now is incredible." But, he laughs, "at least back then, you could always find parking." Maybe it's hard to imagine, considering the traffic jams and parking problems today, but photographs from that period show a sunbaked, nearly desolate Ocean Drive with blocks and blocks of empty parking spaces. There are almost no cars in the pictures. At night, many people were afraid to go out.

But even then, when South Beach looked dark, drugged-out, falling apart, crime-ridden, poverty-stricken, and practically dead, some remarkable people looked at the neighborhood, foresaw a magnificent future, and launched a renaissance. Today, everyone can see that their renaissance succeeded tremendously (though, or course, not perfectly).

But great success did not look particularly inevitable in the beginning, when most local politicians, real estate operators, bankers, and other so-called community leaders had written off the neighborhood and were planning to demolish it. Back in 1976, when a tiny band of preservationists began with a lot of enthusiasm but not much money, their success hardly seemed preordained. Indeed, considering the odds, success was probably not even likely. So how did they do it? How did they save South Beach?

Above: **Designed by Hohauser in 1936 is this sculpted panel on 444 Ocean Drive, another building City Hall wanted to demolish.**
Opposite: **The bright lights of the revived Art Deco district's world-renowned sidewalk café scene on Ocean Drive.**

How South Beach Was Saved

"I love old buildings. But these Art Deco buildings are forty, fifty years old. They aren't historic. They aren't special. We shouldn't be forced to keep them." — Abe Resnick, real estate developer and longtime Miami Beach city commissioner

How does a movement start? Is a great movement in history, like a great wind, caused almost mechanically, simply by a difference in temperature somewhere in the atmosphere?

In history as in weather, does some sort of temperature differential create a low pressure area that a wind must rush in to fill? And in the 1970s, did an enormous temperature differential form in the psychological and economic atmosphere of South Beach? A difference between the cold, almost dead reality of the area's deterioration and the lively, heated enthusiasm that the beautiful but decaying old buildings could still ignite?

Maybe that huge difference — between reality and potentiality — created an economic, social, and aesthetic low-pressure zone, a vacuum in the culture that many people naturally rushed in to fill, like a strong wind.

Or maybe what starts a movement in history is just one great man, or in this case: a great woman.

AND PARTLY LOST

Her name was Barbara Baer Capitman, and she wasn't perfect. In fact, she was damned difficult. At one time or another, she drained and alienated nearly all her friends and allies. But they still loved her. And more than any other single person, she saved South Beach.

In 1976 she encountered South Beach, fell in love with it, and fastened on to the neighborhood. She was fifty-six years

Opposite: **Preparing for a new paint job on the 1941-vintage Carlyle Hotel, workers wield water hoses to blow away pastel layers of paint.** *Above left:* **Fashion photography — including this winter-morning shoot on Ocean Drive — became a major economic factor in South Beach's revival.** *Above right:* **A Rollerblade hero soars in Lummus Park.** *Right:* **Another Deco building goes down: the historic Fifth Street Gym was demolished in 1992 to make room for a parking lot.**

old, a veteran journalist, public relations woman, and specialist in the design field. Her husband, a professor of business and social responsibility, a former UPI reporter, and a pioneer in marketing research, had died the year before, and maybe Capitman was looking for a cause to throw herself into. At the time South Beach was like an enchanted lost city, in pathetic ruins, its beauty dormant. And not everyone could see it under the layers of grime and decay. To most of Miami Beach's business and political establishment, the old 1930s architecture was passé and of little value. To them, the whole neighborhood was a slum and something of an embarrassment.

What Miami Beach's power elite generally wanted then were "modern" high-rise buildings with huge street-level or underground parking garages and hundreds of residential units stacked vertically on a small "footprint" of land. The higher you could build and the more units you could stack, the cheaper the per-unit construction cost and the more profit you could make on the property. Indeed, the more units you could stack, that is, the higher you were allowed by zoning to build, the more valuable your undeveloped land would be — that was the formula. Throw

in deluxe kitchen appliances, a fancy lobby, an impressive-sounding name (The Ocean Club perhaps), and an aggressive advertising campaign declaring the huge building to be "only for the discriminating few" and, it was thought, you could make lots of money by knocking down an old, low-rise building or two and erecting a modern high-rise.

Dozens of high-rises of this sort had been erected in the northern and middle parts of Miami Beach during the 1950s, 1960s, and 1970s, blocking off access to the ocean along middle and upper Collins Avenue with a nearly impenetrable wall of tall, boxy buildings, forming a curiously stark and pedestrian-unfriendly neighborhood that locals called "the Concrete Canyon."

Other developers, meanwhile, had built not vertically but horizontally, sprawling their characterless, automobile-oriented, suburban tract developments and shopping centers onto cheap farm- or swampland in the north, south, and west of the county, often paving over ecologically important wetlands, eating into the Everglades that were crucial to the entire region's water supply, but making lots of money in the process.

That low-rise South Beach was not torn down during this period was an accident of history. Actually, parts of it were. Handsome Mediterranean Revival–style hotels and residences from the '20s that faced Biscayne Bay were replaced by a series of undistinguished apartment towers set in a sea of concrete parking lots. Even the architect of these high-rises on West Avenue, Mel Grossman, disliked them. He called them "filing cabinets for people." He blamed not himself but the city's zoning laws and the developers for whom he worked. "Architects, unfortunately," Grossman told the *Miami Herald* years later, "are victims of the owners' bad taste."

In 1976, the City of Miami Beach passed a redevelopment plan that called for the destruction of virtually every building south of Sixth Street (the southernmost part of South Beach, the area now called South Pointe). Hundreds of small Art Deco and Mediterranean Revival–style buildings — single-family homes, charming low-rise apartment buildings, small oceanfront hotels — virtually everything was supposed to be torn down. About the only thing the planners wanted to save was Joe's Stone Crab Restaurant, a favored dining spot for local politicians, tourists, and businessmen. If implemented, the plan would have displaced thousands of people, many of them elderly and poor. The plan then called for the government to help fund the private development of 2,100 mostly middle- and high-income residential units in medium- and high-rise apartment blocks, plus shopping centers, tennis courts, and hotels on the freshly cleared land. A network of canals was also to be dug, supposedly to transform South Pointe into an American Venice. Fortunately for those who like old buildings, the city never found a mega-developer to implement its grandiose $400-million real estate scheme.

However, many buildings on the western fringe of South Beach and to the north, on Collins, were knocked down throughout the '50s, '60s, and '70s to make room for some ugly but lucrative high-rises. What saved the rest of South Beach?

The old people. Inadvertently, their presence seems to have preserved South Beach; at least they colonized and held the territory long enough to turn the responsibility of saving it over to the preservationists led by Capitman.

Opposite: **In the Concrete Canyon.**

Beginning in the 1950s, when the retirees themselves were younger and relatively affluent, and extending through the 1970s, when so many of the senior citizens had like the buildings themselves become decrepit, these old folks formed enough of an economic and political base to make it worthwhile for the landlords and politicians not to tear the buildings down. Besides, the steadily rotting neighborhood wasn't very attractive, and raw land out by the Everglades was cheaper to develop.

By the time Capitman came on the scene in 1976, however, the aging of South Beach had endangered it. The people were losing their health and vigor; and the buildings were crumbling, making the land on which they stood undervalued, ripe for the taking for some huge, land-intensive development project. Moreover, few in power understood what an asset the old Art Deco buildings were. Indeed, few local business leaders or city officials even understood what the words "Art Deco" meant.

"You know what they used to say?" remembers Deco revival pioneer and Capitman associate Dona Zemo. "'Who's Art?' You know, you'd say, 'This is an Art Deco building,' and they'd say, 'Really, who is Art?' They didn't even know what we were talking about. These people thought 'Art Deco' was some guy's name."

Capitman, on the other hand, was deeply knowledgeable about Art Deco. She'd been introduced to high Deco style back in 1929, when she was nine years old and she and her mother, an industrial designer and sculptress, had sailed to Europe aboard the sleekly Deco, German Moderne luxury liner the S.S. *Bremen.* Among her mother's friends were leading Deco designers, including Raymond Loewy, creator of many classic streamlined consumer products and industrial designs, including the Greyhound bus of the 1940s.

After graduating from New York University with an English degree and working for an Atlantic City newspaper, Barbara began writing and editing for New York–based design magazines in the 1940s. Working in great Art Deco skyscrapers, including the aquamarine-colored, tile-clad McGraw-Hill Building, she edited several magazines, among them *Modern Lighting and Lamps*, and later became Southern editor of one called *The Designer.* She also began a public relations firm with leading designers among her clients, notably Donald Deskey, supervising designer for the interiors of New York's Radio City Music Hall.

With this background, Capitman immediately recognized that the vast array of beat-up buildings she found in South Beach was a treasure. She understood that these old buildings were, in a way, rare collectibles that would only become more valuable with time. And she understood the press and how to get publicity.

But Capitman also had handicaps. She was uncomfortable speaking in public because of her voice: a squeaky, quavering voice mocked by her political opponents, including a loudmouth Miami radio talk-show host who would mimic her on the air. Capitman's peculiar voice resulted partly from the heart and lung problems that eventually killed her. She also had diabetes. She was not a well woman when she embarked on her strenuous fourteen-year crusade to save South Beach from the wrecking ball. Yet she was tireless. She had more energy than any of her helpers, most of them decades younger. Though Capitman was in and out of hospitals constantly during her final years, what kept her alive, say her friends, was not medicine but her work. And though her enemies ridiculed her on the air and at public meetings, they never could silence her.

In 1976 City Hall announced its plan to raze several hundred acres of South Beach. Capitman began organizing. In her first appearance in the news columns of the *Miami Herald*, she sounded her theme: "We believe that tourism would benefit if some of these hotels, which are real treasures, were restored. Instead of tearing down the old hotels, why not put money into interior improvements, paint, landscaping, promenades?"

An early ally was interior designer Edith Irma Siegel, who'd lived and worked in Miami Beach since 1930, designing interiors of homes and big commercial buildings. Siegel was a leader among local designers, and she knew everyone who was anyone.

In 1976, "Barbara came to an American Society of Interior Designers meeting to present her idea. Nobody paid very much attention to her," Siegel recalled years later. "She was not very articulate because of her speech impediment, but she was one of the smartest women I ever met. We were different in every way: she didn't care about her person, how she looked; she wasn't a clotheshorse, but I am...

At any rate, Barbara and I hit it off. We had chemistry immediately. Her object in those days was to see that the retirees who were living there were not put out of their homes; she cared about buildings and people."

Friends would dress Capitman properly for important public appearances, telling her what dress to wear, getting out her pearls, and making sure she got her hair done. Siegel, a stylish, self-made millionairess, owned a black 1966 Rolls-Royce with a red leather interior and often drove Capitman around town in it, lending her a certain credibility and making her arrival at City Hall something of an event. They made an odd pair: Siegel, an elegant and jewel-bedecked size 8; and her pal, Capitman, a stocky and disheveled figure in a tentlike dress and tennis shoes.

Zemo, another close friend, described Capitman as "very down-to-earth, very plain, and very intelligent...an eccentric-looking woman, who, her hair was never, you know — the ocean breeze, she was not fancy. She was not caring to be very well-groomed; she didn't care what people thought about her surface...On the inside, Barbara was very persistent...She didn't stop. She was true blue. I've never met anyone truer to a project than she was...Nothing stopped her."

In June 1976 Capitman and five friends, including Siegel, founded the Miami Design Preservation League. They made up the name while standing on the sidewalk outside 1114 Ocean Drive, a Florida Mediterranean Revival–style villa built in 1930 but modeled after the Dominican Republic palace of Christopher Columbus's son, Diego. Much later, this building on Ocean Drive was purchased by Italian fashion designer Gianni Versace, who renovated it into a sumptuous South Beach palazzo for himself. But that story — including the bitter controversy over Versace's destruction of a neighboring Art Deco building to make room for his private swimming pool — will be told later in this book.

In 1976, one of Capitman's first moves was to start lobbying and educating City Hall. She later wrote proudly, "In 1977, we obtained our first grant: $10,000 from the City Planning Department to conduct a survey and plan for the preservation in Miami

Opposite: **The September 11, 1993, demolition of the Revere, ordered by fashion great Gianni Versace.**

Beach." Capitman and her team would catalog more than 1,200 historic buildings in South Beach. Most were Art Deco, and most stood in a one-square-mile area: the largest concentration of Art Deco buildings in the world. Moreover, the decaying neighborhood still had a stylistic consistency, a coherence that heightened its allure. Hundreds of buildings had been designed by just five or six architects who, working in concert and in competition with one another, had — during an intense, brief period — collectively created a stunning local style that later would be called Tropical Deco. The broken-down neighborhood was a little world unto itself, a town time forgot.

And as far as those in power were concerned, it ought to be torn down. Wrote Capitman in her book *Deco Delights,* "Ocean Drive and all that lay behind it to the West was slated to be Phase II of a plan to revive the Beach by repeating the concrete canyons…the political pattern had been set. The land was too valuable for the small buildings."

Surveying her battlefield, her rich and powerful enemies, and her small but smart band of resistance fighters, General Capitman quickly decided on her first great strategic masterstroke of the war. They could save this town by getting it listed on the National Register of Historic Places, and they would get great press, public awareness, and financial support just by fighting the battle on this high ground. Her opponents fell into the trap by noisily objecting to designating the neighborhood as beautiful, historic, or special. All the big guns came out against it: the Chamber of Commerce, City Hall, the Miami Beach Resort Hotel Association, the Board of Realtors.

Next, Mrs. Capitman went to Washington. Her youngest son, John, recalls the trip: "We roved the halls of Washington with my mother looking more like a bag lady than a well-educated writer." She hauled around "big bags full of materials and pictures…and we would just go door-to-door, trying to get to know people, to talk to them about it." The liberal-activist Carter Administration was in power, and these Democrats liked what the determined little old lady in tennis shoes said about saving the historic architecture and helping the retirees keep their homes. In the New Deal and Great Society tradition, these officials would grant hundreds of thousands of dollars to Capitman's various organizations (she founded several) for her many preservation projects.

The federal officials were also quite ready to make South Beach the first twentieth-century neighborhood to be listed in the National Register of Historic Places. But state approval was also required, and that was where the resistance lay: locally. Capitman's forces and those of her opponents met at a final hearing before a state board.

"After a long, bitter public battle that reached the architectural press and Paul Goldberger in the *New York Times,* the state's Architectural Board of Review voted unanimously," Capitman wrote later. "We joined a packed hall of architectural students and the press in wild, moving cheers…The news went round the world…Approved! The decision signified that a new category of American architecture [Art Deco] was officially part of our heritage. The Empire State Building; Hoover Dam; the Paramount Theater in Oakland, California; the Board of Trade on LaSalle Street in Chicago — all could now take their places with Gettysburg, Monticello, Mount Vernon, and the Alamo, which are listed among America's most historic places…This listing also meant these [South Beach] buildings were now eligible for tax benefits."

A leading South Beach businessman then and now is Joe Nevel. In an interview for this book, he remembered the fight: "The businessmen of Miami Beach looked at Art Deco as a disaster waiting to happen, because they thought it would restrict the demolition of buildings and would discourage development…Primarily, I think they were looking out for their own interests, but they were shortsighted. The elderly were dying off. Their children were going to Europe, Latin America, the Caribbean, for vacations, they were not coming to Miami Beach. It wasn't the hip place to go…It wasn't a particularly attractive prospect: Miami Beach was dying…I was vice president of the Chamber of Commerce the year it was proposed to have the Art Deco Historic District, and the Chamber actually took a vote opposing [it]…I was outvoted. It happened that the following year I became president of the Chamber…I had become very close to Barbara Capitman, she was the godmother of the Art Deco movement down here, and I realized that the only thing the Beach had going for it then, for better or for worse, was the Art Deco movement, and it was suicidal not to support it. I was able to put that view across at my very first meeting as president. We reversed our stand and endorsed the Art Deco movement within a prescribed area."

While winning these battles, Capitman kept organizing on other fronts. In 1978, to bring people to the Beach, she and the League organized the first Art Deco Weekend, a street festival, and the first Moon Over Miami Ball, a fund-raiser complete with a big (if amateur) swing band and held in a rundown hotel on Collins Avenue. It was probably South Beach's first black-tie affair in decades. A couple of hundred people came. Still, Capitman couldn't convince business people to invest in the old buildings. "The numbers won't work," they always said. She needed a pilot project to prove her case.

On Christmas Day, 1978, Andrew Capitman, Barbara's eldest son, signed a contract to buy the Cardozo Hotel for $800,000. Fourteen years later, superstar Cuban-American singer Gloria Estefan and her husband, Emilio, would buy this flowing Streamline Moderne building on glamorous Ocean Drive for a cool $5 million, but back in 1978 the Cardozo was just a dulled 1939 Deco gem in a bad neighborhood.

In 1978, Andrew was only twenty-eight years old and just finishing his Ph.D. in economics. Of course, neither he nor his mother had the required $800,000. "My plan was to float a limited partnership," Andrew said later. "The terms were twenty percent down and the rest was a [seller-financed] mortgage, so I had to raise $160,000 plus working capital…I put out a limited partnership prospectus: thirty-five units of $12,000, to raise about $400,000…You could get some tax benefits, because any losses would be tax deductible. And there was an investment tax credit on any money you spent fixing up [a historic preservation] building…I went out and started selling these units. It was an unbelievable struggle. I was supposed to close by April 15, and by April 15 I hadn't sold any units."

So Capitman bought time: two one-month extensions from the building's seller for $10,000 each. Finally, he managed to close. "I had about $700 left to my name, and I had a pretty neat group of investors," he said later. "So on June 25, 1979, I owned a hotel, and didn't have the vaguest [expletive deleted] idea what to do with it." That same day,

Barbara Baer Capitman at the Cardozo Hotel circa 1979. Photo © Diane Fontayne. Courtesy of the Barbara Baer Capitman Archives, Miami Design Preservation League.

however, an expert sent by the Heritage Conservation and Recreation Service of the U.S. National Parks Service arrived to help guide the hotel restoration — part of a federal program the Capitmans had applied for months before. The advisor's name was Margaret Doyle, and within six months she and Andrew Capitman married.

Together, they went on to make initial restorations of four other major Deco hotels, including the Carlyle and the Victor. But money was a problem. There was never enough to do the job they wanted. The U.S. Department of Commerce had agreed to guarantee a $400,000 loan for restoring the Cardozo. But the twenty-five banks that Andrew Capitman approached all refused to make a loan to any project in slummy South Beach, despite the federal guarantee that the government would repay the loan if Capitman didn't. Eighteen months after they opened the hotel, Capitman finally found a bank to make the federally guaranteed loan. After the Cardozo became something of a success, Capitman was able to raise additional money from private investors to buy more Deco hotels with seller-financed mortgages. But most banks still refused to invest in South Beach. Eventually Andrew Capitman would own and partially restore five Deco hotels, but he never got sufficient loans to restore them completely.

Even so, the Capitmans had started something big. Of course, it wasn't just the Capitmans. Hundreds of other people were part of the movement, among them the husband-and-wife architectural team of Denise Scott-Brown and Robert Venturi, who had proposed an Art Deco historic district as early as 1973. Another key player was a struggling young interior designer named Leonard Horowitz.

Back in their heyday, in the 1930s and 1940s, South Beach's Deco buildings were generally painted white, off-white, or beige. Trim might be painted a contrasting color, brown or dark green perhaps, but mostly the buildings were plain vanilla. It was Barbara Capitman, the writer and organizer, who made Art Deco a household word in the 1980s; but it was Horowitz, the artist and designer, who made Art Deco dazzle.

He "had a mind like a color wheel," wrote the *Miami Herald*. "He would sit in a lawn chair on Ocean Drive and watch the light dance on the buildings," dreaming of highlighting the details and contours with soft yet alluring colors "like adding blush to a cheekbone, gloss to a lip."

First he colorized a fantastic, turreted Deco structure at 685 Washington Avenue that housed a Jewish bakery. Some thought Horowitz crazy, but the pastel peach, periwinkle, white, and sage hues he put on the old building made it look like a confectioner's delight — and put it on the cover of *Progressive Architecture* magazine. In 1982 he received a grant to colorize a whole block of Washington Avenue, and then a commission to "pour pastels onto a bleak block of Fifth Street," as the *Herald* put it. Eventually, some 150 South Beach buildings would be dressed in the color schemes Horowitz created for them.

Capitman called him "my greatest ally," because Horowitz gave South Beach the look: a luscious look that captivated the eyes of the world when his softly pastel-brushed South Beach was showcased in *Miami Vice* (a highly styled mid-1980s TV series with great visuals) and in the exhilarating ads and countless fashion spreads shot by an elite group of photographers who were then gravitating to South Beach.

Above: **Colors by Leonard Horowitz on one of the Beach's earliest Deco masterpieces, the MacArthur Hotel, designed by T. Hunter Henderson in 1930 and now used as an office and commercial building.** *Opposite:* **A fashion photography cliché reenacted again on South Beach.**

If historic movements are indeed caused by some temperature differential in the culture, the photographers, filmmakers, and other artists rushing into South Beach during this period were like molecules of air surging into a low-pressure zone.

William Murray, an English-born photographer then working out of New York, was among the first. Around 1980, the McCann-Erickson advertising agency in New York sent him to South Beach "as a location scout/production guy to see how many neon signs we could find for some Coca-Cola ad. It was all decrepit and burnt-out," he recalled. "At the end of the gig, I stayed

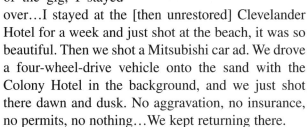

over…I stayed at the [then unrestored] Clevelander Hotel for a week and just shot at the beach, it was so beautiful. Then we shot a Mitsubishi car ad. We drove a four-wheel-drive vehicle onto the sand with the Colony Hotel in the background, and we just shot there dawn and dusk. No aggravation, no insurance, no permits, no nothing…We kept returning there.

"German clients loved Deco, because of the Bauhaus connection [in architectural style], and there was a German photographer called Cheyco Leidman, a lot of his stuff had Miami Beach as a background. And the French mafia [of fashion photographers] was coming down. An English photographer called Willie Christie was doing a lot of English *Vogue* down here…At the time, Miami Beach and Vegas were the two places where European tobacco companies wanted to shoot, those were the two places we were constantly bouncing around.

"A lot of people were coming down for the decay…Some photographers would come and look at the place, and those who didn't have very much vision would say, 'What the hell do I want to shoot down here for? All the hotels are crumbling!'

"But the guys who could really see would say, 'Swing a babe in here in a Gianni Versace skintight outfit and this is going to look OUTRAGEOUS.' Because you had all this passé glamour and sort of rotting neon and old stoops with elderly people on

them…You put some million-dollar babe in front of them and you've got an immediate photograph. You've got yourself a picture!"

As for creature comforts, South Beach was nothing like today. When Murray and his million-dollar models started coming into slummy yet alluring South Beach, there were no good hotels, no hip cafés, no gourmet restaurants. Personally, Murray didn't mind roughing it in the dumpy old hotels, but if his clients came along for the photo shoot, Murray would book them, himself, and his team into one of the big corporate-style hotels over in Coral Gables, or up in the Concrete Canyon, where the hotels didn't particularly appreciate the photo teams, but at least there was room service.

The Cardozo, under the Capitmans' management, was the beginning of the new era. It had a café, the Café Cardozo, which was an instant success when it opened in 1982.

Suddenly you could sit on the veranda of a sleek Art Deco hotel, listen to live jazz or old Frank Sinatra recordings, sip iced cappuccino, and dine on delicacies like marinated scallops. Artists, writers, and architects from mainland neighborhoods like Coconut Grove and Coral Gables began hanging out at the Cardozo. Some even moved into the rooms upstairs. Café Cardozo was also where the photographers and models went.

Dona Zemo, who'd run a Deco-style café in Danbury, Connecticut, heard of the newly restored hotel and came down with a girlfriend for a look. "We were like celebrities," she recalled later. "We were like the first hot visitors to come down and rent an ocean-front room — $40 a day — so Barbara was sort of waiting for us. She was just curious who we were…I met her at the Cardozo and I fell in love with her. I knew of Gertrude Stein and Eleanor Roosevelt and Margaret Meade, but I'd never met any of those great women. Now I felt like I was meeting a great woman."

Barbara Capitman hired Zemo to manage the café. With her extensive show-biz connections, Zemo soon had performers like Patti LaBelle, Eartha Kitt, Lena Horne, and Tommy Tune stopping by the café, while Capitman invited New York artists like Andy Warhol and James Rosenquist to come stay at the hotel and tour the beautiful Historic District. When Christo Javacheff, the media-savvy, Bulgarian-born conceptual artist, came to Miami in 1983 to drape eleven islands in Biscayne Bay with 6.5 million square feet of shimmering pink poly-propylene, he too hung out at Café Cardozo. Christo also took rooms for himself, his family, and his entire crew at two other hotels the Capitmans had reno-vated. And the spectacle of Christo's finished *Surrounded Islands* at-tracted even more of the international art and media crowd to the hotels. Meanwhile, a colony of writers had staked out a regular table at Café Cardozo, and there were still

some old people living upstairs. "It was like this bohemian hotel," said Zemo. "We would all come downstairs and be the people who filled the café, and we would attract the other people. It was like a pyramid."

The pioneers' big problem was that despite the success of the café and hotel, despite all the stunning photos and rhapsodic articles in magazines around the world, despite the international fashion industry's growing love affair with South Beach, the city's power structure continued to allow strategic demoli-tions of beautiful old buildings to make room for the high-rise towers and parking lots that were still, for the most part, the establishment's vision for the future.

Listing South Beach on the National Register of Historic Places had not saved it. The listing was great PR and provided lots of tax incentives for preserva-tion projects, but it still did not legally prohibit someone who bought a historic building from tearing it down. Nor could it prohibit an owner from merely dis-figuring a building by making inappropriate renovations, such as tearing out the won-derful but rotting old interior of the Lincoln Theater instead of re-storing it.

So the pioneers' next great task was to pass a strong local his-toric preservation law to save the endangered buildings. And it was not going to be easy.

In 1980, despite Capitman's strenuous objections, developers bought and then demol-ished the Boulevard Hotel, an elegant seven-story Mediterranean Revival–style structure, constructed in 1925 by pioneer Miami Beach developer Carl Fisher. It had to go, said the new owners, to make room for a sixteen-story condo tower, which, as it turned out, they never built.

More than a decade after the 226-room Boulevard Hotel was demolished, its former site was still a vacant lot. Finally, in 1994, with South Beach now considered a desirable address (due in no small part to the preservationists' efforts), the same real estate developer who tore down the old Boulevard

Above: **South Beach in transition. Many seniors like these were forced out by gentrification.**

and held on to the 1.8-acre site now proposed building on it what the developer called Le Boulevard, a hulking three-building, 180-unit condo complex in a sort of Mediterranean Revival–meets–modern style. This developer was one of the city's most prolific condo builders and probably Capitman's toughest opponent: Abe Resnick.

"It's not that we're trying to tear down a historical monument," Resnick had said back in 1980 when he and his partners ordered the old Boulevard demolished. "You just can't keep it up. It's too old. The thing is falling down. It has to come down." That was his theme, repeated again and again, about building after building. They had to come down.

In 1981 Resnick and partners publicly announced plans to preserve and renovate the New Yorker Hotel, a splendidly streamlined Art Deco oceanfront hotel built in 1940 and considered by many to be a masterpiece. But unexpectedly Resnick and his partners switched signals and said they would tear the building down. "Why is it so important?" asked Resnick. "George Washington never slept there." Private ownership meant they could destroy it, explained one of Resnick's partners, adding that if they owned the *Mona Lisa,* ownership would give them the right to destroy that, too.

Capitman organized vigils and demonstrations at the hotel, getting tremendous media coverage of the controversy, but she couldn't stop the wrecking ball, and the sleek hotel went down. Afterward Resnick blamed the New Yorker's demise on his partners, saying, "This happened when I was away in Europe."

More than a decade later, however, Resnick admitted he'd ordered the demolition because he figured the New Yorker was worth only about $20,000, while the beachfront property on which it stood was potentially worth millions. "There are a couple dozen buildings worth preserving," Resnick once said of South Beach. "For the rest of them, this is a waste of time, making studies." In 1981 the City Commission, which is the city's legislature, agreed, defeating a preservationist proposal to impose a moratorium on demolitions in the historic district.

Just as Capitman alone was not the entire preservation movement (she had hundreds of colleagues), Resnick alone was not the entire opposition. He also had hundreds of like-minded people with him. But it is hard not to personalize the great battle for the soul of South Beach as the battle between these two powerful personalities: Capitman and Resnick.

"She found some kind of beauty in these ugly buildings, but I don't see it," Resnick told a reporter in 1981. "I have trouble grasping what this is about, what drives her."

And what drove Resnick? Born Abraham Resnickowitz in Lithuania, he was seventeen years old in 1941 when his parents, his two sisters, and some 3,200 other Jews in his hometown were massacred by the invading German Army. Young Resnick was away at school in the provincial capital Kovno at the time, but was soon captured by the Nazis and pressed into slave labor. Among other things, he was forced to repair German airfields after they were bombed. He and five other prisoners hoarded some bread, sugar, and water, watched the movements of the guards, and then cut through the barbed wire and escaped.

But outside the city, they were stopped at a checkpoint. They had no papers, so they ran. Each ran by prearrangement in a different direction. One was shot, while according to accounts Resnick gave later, the other four escaped. Resnick hid in a cornfield, then fled into a dark forest where he wandered several days, eating leaves to survive and covering himself with grass to keep warm at night. Hungry and cold, he stumbled upon some escaped Russian prisoners of war, who gave him a knife. Together, they eventually joined resistance fighters in the forest and sabotaged rail lines using weapons Russian planes airdropped along with instructions. Fluent in Russian, German, and Lithuanian, Resnick was pressed into the Russian Army as an interpreter and was with the Red Army when it took Berlin.

After the war, Lt. Resnick wanted out of the Red Army. His only surviving family were in Havana, so that was his destination. He defected and managed to reach Paris, where he bought false identity papers, then fled to North Africa and from there to Cuba. He worked as a laborer in Havana, in his uncle's textile factory, and studied Spanish at night. With $500 he managed to borrow, Resnick opened a butcher shop in Havana and parlayed that into a Cuban real estate empire. By the time Castro took Havana, Resnick was a rich man.

Again, Resnick fled an invading army. He fled to Miami and started all over again. He learned English and he worked hard. In 1963 he bought his first property on Miami Beach, a lot on Eleventh Street, and

built an eight-unit apartment house there. Again starting from the bottom, he built an empire; eventually he owned some seventy Miami Beach properties.

The *Miami Herald* described the dozens of South Beach apartment houses Resnick built as "1960s utilitarian, squat…two or three stories high." Instead of the wealth of interesting facades, sculpted panels, and decorative door treatments that the older Deco apartment buildings presented to pedestrians, Resnick's buildings typically offered merely a ground-level parking garage to look at.

Resnick ran his empire from a small office above

a hardware store on Alton Road. And like a lot of developers, he squeezed as many units into his buildings as the law allowed.

So this was Resnick, Capitman's archenemy: a tough, brilliant, and almost unstoppable survivor. A fighter. In person, he was a wiry, compact, energetic man with a quick smile, a strong handshake, and a

Above: **Abe Resnick in 1995, at age seventy-one, in the library of his Miami Beach home.** *Opposite:* **A mainly gay section of the beach has developed from about Twelfth to Thirteenth Streets.**

certain elegance in his bearing. And he didn't like people telling him what to do. "I had been a slave" under the Nazis and Russians, he said in an interview for this book. "I didn't have any rights. Now I am in this country of democracy and human rights, and, you know, some property owners' rights...Barbara Capitman came on very strong: You cannot do this! You cannot do that!...I was resenting that she would come and try to impose on me this and this and that."

With the dramatic decline of the neighborhood caused by the aging of the retirees, the decay of many old buildings, and the influx of Third World refugees and immigrants, Resnick must have known the value of his South Beach properties was declining. And like many other hard-driving businessmen at the time, he reckoned the answer was to tear down the old buildings — which he thought were unattractive — and build high-rises.

"I really don't find any beauty" in Art Deco, he said at the time. "But it might be I'm shortsighted. Maybe I need glasses, rose-colored glasses."

Many other leading businessmen shared his blind spot. For instance, in 1981 Murray Gold, executive director of the Miami Beach Resort Hotel Association, declared, "No one in their right mind just walks around and looks at old buildings...People want to see new things. They don't like to see the old."

For the next decade or so, the battle in South Beach would be largely over these two things: educating the establishment, and enacting strong enough local laws to prevent uncomprehending developers from destroying the historic district. Along the way, some great buildings would be saved and some would be lost. Through it all, the battle between Resnick and Capitman continued.

In 1983, Capitman, disgusted by City Hall, decided to run for City Commission. Her campaign

buttons featured a pink flamingo; her slogan was "Think Pink" (a favorite Horowitz color, of course); and her idea of a political fund-raiser was a masked ball at a Deco hotel. In the election she received 2,551 votes, finishing, in a field of five, dead last.

Winning her district, receiving 5,226 votes, was a university administrator who had advocated giving developers big government incentives to build new hotels.

Capitman lost that election, but she and the Preservation League were still winning the cultural war. Their annual Art Deco Weekend had grown into a huge three-day Ocean Drive street festival, jazz concert, costume ball, Deco film festival, and educational extravaganza held every January. By the middle of the decade, the event was drawing hundreds of thousands of people to the Art Deco Historic District. Jazz artists with roots in the Swing Era, including Cab Calloway, Lionel Hampton, and Dizzy Gillespie, performed in the park beside Ocean Drive; art and antiques were sold at little booths on the street; and historical displays, Art Deco lectures, and urban planning seminars were held in the old buildings.

Artists, hip entrepreneurs, gay people, and other trendsetters were moving to the Beach. Each month there were more renovations, more restaurants, more cafés, and more boutiques, though the neighborhood was still tough and bohemian, a funky mixture of old and young, immigrants and artists. An underground nightlife was beginning, with parties held in abandoned buildings, and strange new nightclubs were appearing.

Meanwhile, beginning in 1984, the *Miami Vice* TV series did more than showcase the new South Beach; it also helped subsidize it by pouring millions of dollars into the neighborhood.

Locations were rented. (One favorite was the late-1930s-style lobby of the Victor Hotel that the

Capitmans and other preservationists had restored.) Local actors got work; caterers were hired to feed the crew; hotel rooms were booked; equipment was rented; and nightclubs were busy. *Miami Vice* even paid some owners to repaint their buildings in the pastel hues for which the hit show and the town were becoming famous.

Around the same time, on still-blighted Lincoln Road, a potter named Ellie Schneiderman rented (and later, with government grants, bought) several buildings that she turned into low-rent, government-subsidized studios for artists. More than anything else, this saved Lincoln Road, then a nearly dead pedestrian mall with more than one hundred of its storefronts empty.

"The Fifth Avenue of the South" had fallen so far that homeless people used the doorways of the abandoned shops as their bedrooms and latrines. Yet the outline of the street's beauty was still there. The artists were the urban pioneers who resettled this tough territory, fixing up many an old building, not only on Lincoln Road but in the dilapidated Deco residential neighborhoods nearby. On Lincoln Road

there began to appear boutiques and galleries with names like Godzilla and Hyperspace.

Among the pioneering artists who came into Schneiderman's South Florida Art Center were Stewart Stewart and his wife Dena, who decided to liven up Lincoln Road still further by erecting a movie screen in the street, selling popcorn, and showing silent movies once a week to the accompaniment of a pianist who played for tips. On movie nights the galleries and boutiques stayed open late, and people began coming to Lincoln Road again.

During 1984 and 1985 some local officials and business leaders were moving toward the preservationist position. Perhaps the turning point came when the city's new planning director urged the preservation of the Ocean Drive hotels in particular and Art Deco in general. This plan eventually prevailed, and among other things, the city widened the sidewalk on Ocean Drive. At the time it was not wide enough for two people to walk abreast without hitting a parking

Above: **Stewart Stewart by Stewart Stewart with Stewart Stewart.** *Opposite:* **Party time!**

38

meter or utility pole. The city tripled the width of the sidewalks from five to fifteen feet and passed laws allowing sidewalk cafés. Lummus Park, which runs beside Ocean Drive, linking it to the beach, was spruced up, and the state spent millions widening the beach itself.

But other major jobs remained. Most important was getting the city to protect the buildings by passing a strong historic preservation law.

In 1985 Resnick, long a power behind the scenes, ran for a city commission seat. At this point, Resnick was soft-pedaling his antipreservation past. "I've always been in favor of it [Art Deco]," he told the *Herald.* "I think it's fabulous."

Capitman loudly denounced Resnick's candidacy. But a mutual friend invited them to lunch at Wolfie's, South Beach's most famous Jewish delicatessen, and brokered a deal. "Bagel diplomacy," exclaimed the *Miami Herald,* hailing what it called "The Wolfie Accords." Essentially, the deal was that Resnick would support historic preservation in general and an Art Deco educational center in particular (one of Capitman's pet projects); and in exchange Capitman was to endorse Resnick's candidacy. Resnick won his seat on the City Commission, but the Wolfie Accords didn't last long.

WAR DECLARED ON AGAIN was the new headline in the *Herald.* Capitman had called a press conference and denounced her nemesis for, she said, breaking his word. The City Planning Board was considering a preservation law to protect historic buildings on Ocean Drive and Collins Avenue. But Resnick, who had several properties there, was maneuvering to exclude them from the law by getting a half-block of Collins, which included the Sands Hotel, dropped from the law, and then by asking the board to drop all of Collins from the preservation law, in effect cutting the size of the preservation district in half.

This was war, all right. Capitman went ballistic. For these hotels "to be destroyed, to be ruined by this single-minded, petty greed and bad taste is too serious to ignore," she thundered. Resnick shot back that her press conference was just a publicity stunt. Ultimately, the Sands, which stood next to where the Resnick-demolished New Yorker had been, was also demolished to make a bigger site for the high-rise hotel, which many in power still wanted. Proponents said that the city and its then-money-losing convention center needed a big, modern, corporate-style hotel, not just little renovated Deco ones that might be too funky for business travelers or too bohemian for the middle-American tourists.

Meanwhile, the always undercapitalized Andrew Capitman lost control of his five Art Deco hotels when his investors accepted a large buyout offer. The new owner, the Royale Group, had Atlantic City connections and wanted to bring casino gambling to South Beach. Royale's chief executive, Leonard Pelullo, made the Carlyle Hotel on Ocean Drive a popular place but got embroiled in a series of nasty legal problems. He was accused in a civil suit of raiding the pension fund of a New Jersey printing company and was briefly jailed until he paid back the missing $1.7 million. Later he was acquitted in Ohio of charges that he paid a

kickback to a savings and loan president to get a $1 million loan. In California he was convicted of forty-nine counts of wire fraud and one count of racketeering for allegedly misappropriating $2.2 million in loans from another S&L, and was sentenced to twenty-four years. However, an appeals judge overturned those convictions on the grounds that certain FBI and bank documents were wrongly admitted into evidence. In another case, a trucking company Pelullo partly owned was accused of failing to pay $3.9 million in back taxes. Later, a New Jersey Commission of Investigation report on professional boxing alleged Pelullo was "a key organized crime associate" and linked his family to that of Philadelphia crime boss Angelo Bruno, allegations Pelullo denied. He sued the commission for libel, but a judge later dismissed the suit. A few years later, in 1995, Pelullo was convicted in Philadelphia of one count of racketeering and forty-six counts of wire fraud.

Sometime in the middle of all this, Pelullo's Royale Group lost ownership of its Art Deco hotels — but not before it tore one down, the Senator, to make room for a ground-level parking lot.

It was Capitman's last great fight. For nineteen months the preservationists forestalled the Senator's demolition. "Vigils, appeals to the city, parades, phone calls, letters, and incredible round-the-clock coverage by radio and TV kept the Senator standing," she wrote enthusiastically in early 1988. But that autumn, Pelullo's company decided to tear down the forty-nine-year-old Deco building. Though she was

Opposite: **The Berkeley Shore Hotel at 1610 Collins Avenue, designed in 1940 by Albert Anis and photographed some fifty-four years later.** *Above:* **One of the dozens of surviving Deco screen doors in South Beach, this one had been broken but was recently restored. Hundreds have been lost.**

in failing health, Capitman organized several candle-light vigils, personally staying overnight on the old building's porch. Ever-conscious of the media, Capitman donned a flowing black garment that she called the "robes of justice" and chained herself to one of the building's pillars. She was wearing her robes when police hauled her off the porch before the cameras; and the building was reduced to rubble.

As always, when she lost a building, Capitman gained worldwide sympathy for her cause; but she still lost a building, and her health was going, too. After the Senator, she was in and out of hospitals a lot. She also lost leadership of the Miami Design Preservation League that she had founded. There's a lot of controversy over how that happened and why. "Groups of people would come in," said her son, John. "Here was this frail, old lady with the screechy, squeaky voice, and they got the idea she could just be pushed aside and they could take [the League] in the direction they wanted."

Part of the power struggle involved differences over the League's direction, but it was also about personalities. Barbara could be difficult with even her best friends. "I didn't talk to her for a year," said her old comrade, Dona Zemo. "She was so demanding, and she drove me so nuts…She got so out of control that she was gone. She was like possessed by Art Deco."

Financial crises pursued Capitman. "Like a locomotive engineer stripping all the wood from his railroad cars to feed the furnace and keep the train going, the Miami Design Preservation League began giving up its fixtures one by one to meet its office bills," wrote historian Howard Kleinberg about one crisis. "Out went the air conditioning, out went the copying machine, eight desks, two filing cabinets…Capitman remained optimistic: 'We'll get help [she said], we've been in this situation a couple of times before.'"

When she needed something, she wouldn't take no for an answer. And however much you gave her, she wanted more. She always needed money. At one point, remembers painter Stewart Stewart, "She felt that she should get a fee from everybody who exploited the district: photographers, hotels, everything; she felt she should get a piece of everything, because she made the district."

This concept was poorly received, especially by all the people who felt they, too, had helped make the district. But it wasn't that Capitman was being greedy for herself. She lived modestly, but she needed money for her projects. She had begun another crusade: to save the endangered, Arabian Nights–like Moorish Revival architecture of Opa-locka, a Miami suburb of the 1920s that by the 1980s had become one of America's poorest towns. She also founded a short-lived magazine; wrote a book, *Deco Delights,* about South Beach; and helped form or advised Art Deco societies in numerous other cities, including Boston and Washington. She and her closest colleagues also organized the First World Congress on Art Deco, held in South Beach, to promote awareness of the Deco style in Australia, Indonesia, South America, Canada, and other regions, as well as in the United States. Meanwhile the Reagan Administration had slashed federal funding for historic preservation projects, so financing all this was harder than ever. To try to make ends meet, Capitman started up her PR agency again.

Though she was low on funds, the Deco Revival that she and Andrew, now an investment banker in New York, had begun was finally booming. New entrepreneurs with more experience and better financing were doing dozens of beautiful and important South Beach projects, and were wielding some clout at City Hall. Among the new wave were Tony Goldman, whose beautiful renovations of the Park Central and Imperial hotels on Ocean Drive are only part of his portfolio; Craig, Scott, and Stacy Robins of DACRA Development, who did brilliant jobs with some of the hotels Capitman once owned plus many other properties; and Chris Blackwell, the legendary Jamaican-born movie and international pop music mogul (Bob Marley, Grace Jones, U2, and King Sunny Ade), whose Marlin Hotel is on the cover of this book.

Meanwhile Lenny Horowitz, who'd created the popular pastel color scheme for much of South Beach and who was like a third son to Barbara, died of AIDS in 1989. Capitman was dying, too. Her heart was failing, her lungs were filling with fluid, and there were many complications. She was in and out of hospitals, and she knew she was dying. Her youngest son, John, a gerontologist, helped make her last months as productive as possible by vetoing back operations and other medical interventions her doctors had prescribed.

She worked feverishly on another book, *Rediscovering Art Deco U.S.A.,* with her longtime friends Michael Kinerk and Dennis Wilhelm. They didn't realize just how close to death she was, but she knew. An hour before she died, Wilhelm complimented her about a big article in that morning's *Miami Herald* about her and the district. Her reply: Wait till you see the one tomorrow.

According to her son, John, "The afternoon my mom lost consciousness, I was sitting with her. She was hooking up a new computer. I was showing her how to use WordPerfect and then she dictated a press release for someone; she still needed [to do PR work] to make money. And then she got so excited about the printer working, she had to go lie down. And that was really the end of her life."

Barbara Baer Capitman died on March 29, 1990, a week before her seventieth birthday.

During her last days she had given a series of dramatic interviews from her deathbed to different reporters, and the day she died she was quoted in the *Herald* as saying, "These buildings are in more danger now than they ever were," referring to some new high-rise plan. And just as she predicted, the next day there was an even bigger story about her beloved buildings and her struggle to save them. It was her obituary on page one.

A couple of days later, a columnist made public what was probably her last interview. In it she said, "Every preservationist should be at the battlements. It is not the time for division…This is not the time for compromise."

Family and friends had planned a big seventieth birthday party for Capitman, and they went ahead with it anyway, figuring that's what she would have wanted.

In appreciation for all she'd done for the city she

Opposite: **A vintage sign on a 1940 Dixon building, the Beachway Apartments, 701 Fourteenth Street.**

loved, her admirers also asked the Miami Beach City Commission to make some memorial to her: name a major street after her, or a plaza, or maybe even turn an old Art Deco building into that community and educational center she'd always wanted. The commission dismissed all these proposals, but rather grudgingly agreed to rename one small block of Tenth Street, between Ocean Drive and Collins Avenue, Barbara Capitman Way — and even that was opposed by Resnick, who said, "I think that's over-

doing it."

But Resnick repented later. In 1994 he attended a conference in Tel Aviv about saving that city's many endangered Deco-like buildings, and said, "I learned that a city could be brought together by an art movement. Basically I have to recognize that I'm quite more educated about the Art Deco [now]. I should have listened to the lady in the tennis shoes."

As for the New Yorker, Resnick said, "I wish I had it today. Today it would be worth a fortune."

BOOM AND BUST ON A BILLION-DOLLAR SANDBAR

"Swamp and mangrove trees so thick that a man could not get through without an axe to cut his way." — South Beach's first developer, J. N. Lummus, describing the property

Searching for the Fountain of Youth, Juan Ponce de Leon discovered Florida by mistake on Easter Sunday, 1513. He named the new land La Florida after a Spanish phrase for the Easter season, "Pascua Florida," the Feast of Flowers.

The tale is too good not to tell — and it's at least partly true. It's certainly true that Ponce, an experienced soldier, was searching for a rich island Caribbean Indians had described to him and which he hoped to exploit. The name part is mostly true, too; at least it appears in Ponce's log, according to a summary written some ninety years later. Ponce actually landed a few days after Easter Sunday, but still during the Feast of Flowers, and he indeed christened his new world La Florida.

But it's likely that La Florida had already been discovered by two English explorers and some Spanish slave hunters.

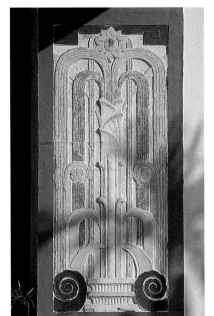

Still, it is Ponce who claims the great peninsula for Spain. And forever claims the heart of the traditional story, for it resonates with a deep mythic quality of archetypal symbols: a new world, a blossoming of flowers, a feast, a knight, a quest, a magic fountain, a resurrection.

The unforgettable legend of a fountain of youth was already an old tale told a million times, with a thousand different heroes, in Europe and the Middle East before Ponce was grafted onto the myth and made its quest knight in a couple of early Spanish accounts, one written in a sensationalistic, almost tabloid tone.

The Indians had no fountain myth. But a conquistador discovering a New World and encountering alien civilizations was nearly as sensational to sixteenth-century Europeans as an

This page: **The flowing fountain motif on a bas-relief on the Charles Hotel.**

astronaut discovering a new planet in space and encountering alien civilizations would be to us today — and some writers and publishers probably took advantage of public interest in the big story and tarted it up a bit, just as some writers for supermarket tabloids, TV movies, or of quickie books would today.

But however apocryphal the search for the Fountain of Youth may be, the story will never die, because the search for new worlds, for new beginnings, to be born again, to find immortality, and to be forever young appeals to something deep in us. Through its sheer charm and deep appeal, plus rote repetition by writers and historians, the age-old fountain myth has fastened itself so firmly into the texture of Florida history that it can probably never be excised. Thus, the magic fountain that never was has made Ponce immortal after all. His story lives forever young as every schoolchild to whom it is taught.

In any event, Don Juan Ponce de Leon, the Spanish-born governor of Puerto Rico, had landed somewhere on the east coast of Florida, probably near Cape Canaveral, though the City of St. Augustine insists on claiming the honor. The conquistador then sailed down the coast to what is now Miami. According to archaeologists, a small Indian settlement stood near the mouth of the Miami River.

Fast-forward now nearly four centuries, skipping over the imperial wars between the Spanish, French, English, and eventually the Americans; the colonization of Florida and the First and Second Seminole Wars; General (later President) Andrew Jackson and the broken treaties; the genocide; the pioneers; the alligators; the exploitation: the usual.

Modern Miami history, and the prodigious boom-and-bust cycle that typifies it, opens in 1896 with the arrival in Miami of Rockefeller financial wizard Henry Flagler's railroad, another magical opening of a new world. The first tourists arrive on Flagler's train the very next year to vacation at his new and deluxe Royal Palm Hotel, described by a newspaper as "a huge, yellow-and-white board structure wrapped in cool verandas, set in a green tropical park near the mouth of the Miami River." Then, as now, the area's prime attraction was its sunny, warm winter weather.

At this point Miami was little more than an Indian trading post and booming frontier town in a tropical wilderness. In the late 1890s Florida was as much a frontier as the American West had been twenty years earlier. As for Miami Beach, it could be reached only by boat and was still mostly uninhabited swamp, half underwater, infested by alligators, and covered by deep tropical jungle. Except in South Beach, where a handful of pioneers had cleared some land.

Most of what is now South Beach had been purchased from the state of Florida for 35 cents an acre in 1881. The buyer was a Pennsylvania farmer named Henry Lum, who planned to make a fortune growing coconuts on his new plantation (everything south of what is now Fourteenth Street). His son and daughter-in-law became South Beach's first settlers, building a two-story thatched-roof wooden house in the wilderness (at what is now Ocean Drive and Twelfth Street). There they ate sea turtle egg omelets, oyster stew, fresh fish, and game they caught, plus chickens they raised and vegetables from their

Above: **Another fountain, a key Art Deco motif, especially apropos in Ponce de Leon's Florida.**
Opposite: **Beachgoers buy fast food where pioneers gathered sea turtle eggs just a century before.**

garden. But their coconut plantation failed (rats, rabbits, and raccoons ate most of the coconut seeds before they could grow into trees); and the Lums left after eight years on the island.

About this time, another group, including a New Jersey horticulturist named John Collins, bought a huge tract north of Lum's and planted more coconuts. But the jungle was too dense, the mosquitos too fierce; and ultimately this plantation, too, failed. A few fishermen's shacks remained, and some Miami businessmen built on the beach, near the southern tip of the island, what were called "bathing casinos": basically bathhouses, where visitors who came by boat from the mainland (20 cents round-trip) could change into their modest bathing attire. One place, a two-story building called Dick Smith's Casino, also boasted a little refreshment stand and a small dance floor — evidently South Beach's first nightclub.

In 1907 a seventy-year-old Collins returned to Miami Beach to give agriculture another go. This time the stubborn old man planted pear, banana, and mango trees, plus tomatoes, corn, peppers, and potatoes. His investors included two Miami bankers, the brothers J. E. and J. N. Lummus (pronounced "Loomis"). They lent Collins money; but more importantly, they grasped the island's potential for residential development.

In 1912 the Lummus brothers bought all the land south of what is now Lincoln Road — and launched South Beach's first real estate boom. Already, prices were skyrocketing.

Thirty years earlier Lum paid 35 cents an acre for his plantation, but "We paid from $150 per acre to $12,500 per acre for swampland," J. N. Lummus wrote. "The large price was paid for small tracts, but we had to have them to put the streets through."

They immediately hired a small army of laborers to chop down the jungle that blanketed the island. But they found that the jungle harbored many creatures.

"We killed seventeen of the largest rattlesnakes south of Fifteenth Street," wrote Lummus. "When you kill one, tie it to a stake and another one will be coiled there the next morning." There were other pests: "Coons by the hundreds," complained Lummus, adding, "My son, Tom, and I, with my old dog, Black Joe, caught and killed" the raccoons. Worst of all, perhaps, South Beach was also plagued in 1912 with "rats by the thousands." So Lummus

advertised in the Miami newspapers for cats, and readers sent him bags of cats. "They cleaned up the rats," wrote Lummus gratefully. To this day, hundreds of alert though raggedy alley cats still roam South Beach, perhaps descendants of those bagfuls of felines who once rescued South Beach from the rats (at least from the four-legged kind).

Still no bridge existed, so the Lummuses purchased a ferry boat service and cut the fares. Now, for just a nickel, you could take a boat from downtown Miami and cross the crystal-clear bay to the western shore of Miami Beach. From a wooden landing there, ladies in their bonnets and gentlemen in their derbies walked across the island on a boardwalk built above the swamp at what is now Biscayne Street. By the ocean side, visitors found the Lummus brothers' bathing casino. The nickel boat ride "was so popular that some of the people rode back and forth all day," wrote J. N., adding, "Of course, the five cent fare did not pay for the operation of the boats, but the difference was made up in the sale of lots to visitors." He had his salesmen on the boats.

And this was just the beginning. The Lummus brothers and Collins joined forces to build a wooden bridge across the bay. Unfortunately, there were unexpected costs and they ran out of money, with their uncompleted bridge across Biscayne Bay stuck in the water, a tantalizing half-mile from the island. People called it "Collins' Folly."

Enter Carl Fisher. He was an Indiana farmboy who rose from racing bicycles to racing cars professionally with hero driver Barney Oldfield, with whom he staged two-man car races. They made a ton of money barnstorming the Midwest together; and although Fisher's eyesight was poor, he set a world speed record in 1904, piloting a car to nearly sixty miles an hour. Capitalizing on the publicity, young Fisher opened pioneering car dealerships in the Midwest and promoted them with ever-more-spectacular publicity stunts, such as personally flying over Indianapolis in the driver's seat of a sparkling white automobile that he had suspended from a large crimson hot air balloon. Carl Fisher knew how to get people's attention.

He was only nineteen when he opened his first car dealership, and was a millionaire by the time he was twenty-three. With a partner, Fisher bought the patents for the first really bright automobile headlamps and organized the Prest-O-Lite company to manufacture them. However, until the process was perfected, his factories (which compressed carbide gas for the lamps to burn) had a nasty habit of blowing up. Despite such unfortunate incidents in Bayonne, New Jersey, and Omaha, Nebraska (news of which Fisher tried to suppress), he made a fortune

Roosevelt. Together they lobbied federal, state, and local governments to build a series of paved roads that connected coast to coast: America's first paved cross-country route. Fisher called it the Lincoln Highway and coined the slogan "See America First."

When he was thirty-five years old, the irrepress-

with the Prest-O-Lite lamp, the first to make night driving practical. Next, in 1909, Fisher built the oval Indianapolis Speedway and began promoting car races, but attendance was poor until 1911, when Fisher dreamed up and ballyhooed a 500-mile car race, a spectacular endurance contest for men and machines. He called it the Indianapolis 500. It's still run on the brick-paved, 3.2-mile Speedway every Memorial Day, an American classic. But this was just a warmup to Fisher's bigger accomplishments. He is responsible for America's first transcontinental highway. At this time, outside of the cities there were few paved roads, and automobile travel was arduous and adventurous. To encourage car sales, Fisher organized a coalition of early car manufacturers and cement and tire companies, plus some of his personal friends, such as Thomas Edison and Teddy

ible Fisher met and married a pretty, fifteen-year-old, Indianapolis schoolgirl named Jane Watt. Like most Indiana youngsters, she idolized Fisher, then the Hoosier State's richest, most famous, and most daring young man. Three years later, after he sold Prest-O-Lite to Union Carbide for $9 million, Carl and Jane came to vacation in Miami. It was January 1912.

Fisher liked speedboats, and sometimes he and his friends explored by boat the brackish waterways that crisscrossed the then swampy island of Miami Beach. "Blue hyacinths impeded their progress,"

Above: **Many think bicycles are the best way to get around South Beach today.** *Overleaf:* **The Twelfth Street lifeguard shack, designed by architect Bill Lane.**

wrote Jane in her memoirs. "Vines and mangrove and the bristly little palmettoes made dark colonnades."

On one such visit to the island, Fisher met a short, soft-spoken, elegantly dressed old man in a clearing in the wilderness: John Collins. Impressed that anyone so old would embark on such grand plans for the island, Fisher lent him and the Lummus brothers $50,000 to complete their bridge, in exchange for some of their land.

"When later we went by boat to inspect the new property, I protested," wrote Jane. "What on earth could Carl possibly see in such a place, I wondered crossly as I picked my way through the morass in my white shoes…

"An old alligator roared its resentment…mosquitoes blackened our white clothing…the mosquitoes were biting every exposed inch of me…the jungle itself was as hot and steamy as a conservatory…I refused to find any charm in this deserted strip of ugly land. But Carl was like a man seeing visions. He had pulled a stick and peeled it…and when we reached the clean sand, he drew upon it a plan of

Above: **The Tenth Street lifeguard shack by architect Bill Lane and pop artist Kenny Scharf, both based in South Beach.** *Opposite:* **Floridiana for sale at the Miami Design Preservation League's annual Art Deco Weekend, every January.**

streets…It was Carl's greatest and craziest dream," wrote Jane. The land they had traversed was where Fisher would build Lincoln Road.

"Carl sent in hundreds of Negroes with machetes to clear the jungle. Foot by foot, their backs dripping with sweat, they hacked their way through," Jane tells us. A period photo shows a black laborer almost dwarfed by huge above-ground mangrove roots and the towering mangrove trees themselves. And incredibly hard to remove were the palmettos, low, dense tropical plants with huge, thick, bladelike leaves radiating from their tough green trunks. Even mules with chains and grappling hooks could not uproot them. In his frustration, Fisher would attack the plants personally, pulling at the stubborn roots with his bare hands, but of course to no avail. Finally, Fisher asked one of his automobile industry friends to build an enormous steel plow that, pulled by an early tractor, did the job.

Next, Fisher and the Lummuses, who'd allied to develop the land, had to fill in the swamps. On huge barges, they floated into the bay with noisy dredging machines that sucked up six million cubic yards of bay bottom. Laborers mixed this thick bay-bottom soil with palmetto leaves and mangrove wood from the clear-cutting. They poured this mixture into the swamps. The developers put $600,000 — perhaps $4 million in today's money — into what was Florida's first dredge-and-fill operation. But to their horror, after six months in the baking Florida sun the heavy bay-bottom muck, acquired at such great cost, dried out and turned into snow-white sand that began blowing away. There were sandstorms. The developers had turned a jungle into a desert.

Not a blade of swamp grass nor hardly any trees had been left alive to hold the soil. The developers

hastily imported new topsoil and fertile muck from the Everglades. Eager schoolboys hired by the Lummus brothers planted strong-rooted Bermuda grass on 500 acres, earning 10 cents an hour and free swims in the ocean, while on his land Fisher hired "hundreds of Negroes, most of them women and children" to plant grass, orchid trees, poincianas, hibiscus, oleanders, royal palms, and orange and lemon trees. Within six months, the island blossomed. Wrote Jane Fisher, "Overnight, our man-made paradise was discovered by choruses of singing birds and brilliant clouds of butterflies."

Unfortunately, added J. N. Lummus in his memoirs, "We also had millions of mosquitoes, and I, as mayor, wrote our Florida representatives in Washington…The government sent us the men who cleaned up the mosquitoes on the Panama Canal." They rid Miami Beach of most of its thirty-two species of mosquitoes. "We offered to pay the government," continued Lummus, "but no charge was made."

Fisher, meanwhile, was planning what he called an "American Riviera" on Miami Beach. When he laid out Lincoln Road he told his men, "Make it wide. Make the goddamn street one hundred feet wide! I tell you Lincoln Road is going to be the American Rue de la Paix." They lined the street with stately palms and laid a roadbed of brilliant crushed white coral.

The Fisher-financed bridge opened in 1913. The tolls were 5 cents round-trip for a pedestrian; 20 cents for a horse and rider; and 30 cents for a two-horse wagon or a lightweight motorcar. The wooden boards of the bridge were loose and clattered for the entire two-and-a-half mile trip across the bay.

The Lummus brothers then declared they'd give away free lots on beautiful Atlantic (now Collins) Avenue to the first twenty-five people who'd build homes there. They got takers from all over the United States, and in 1914 the Lummuses actually gave away lots to help kick off the Beach's first building boom. The property would be worth millions today. The Lummus brothers also bought cheap chinaware

Opposite: **Lummus Park during the annual Miami Beach International Kite Festival. The lizard-shaped kite in the background is nearly eighty feet long and was designed by Peter Lynn of New Zealand.**

by the railroad carload and hired a silver-tongued salesman named Edward E. "Doc" Dammers to give the stuff away to everyone who'd come to the great Lummus land auctions. At their first auction, in February 1912, even before the bridge was open, some 300 people gathered on the sand at the southern tip of South Beach, where Doc stood on the backboard of a mule-drawn wagon.

"To see Doc Dammers in action," wrote Lummus, "was worth the money. After sizing up the people and giving them a real sales talk on the future possibilities of this Ocean Heaven for the Sun Seeker, he would reach in the hat and draw out a number. Each passenger on every boat had a number," and each won something. In between the giveaways, Doc auctioned off fifty-foot lots in South Beach for about $1,100 each.

The Fishers looked down their noses at such tactics. "The sales method of a big tent barker," sniffed Jane. "Carl scorned to offer plated silverware or flowered washbowls." However, Fisher's Miami Beach land wasn't selling too well yet, and he eventually also hired Doc Dammers and gave away some free land to start the ball rolling. In the end, though, Fisher's most effective sales method was actually to raise his prices and market his part of Miami Beach as a lavish and "exclusive" resort for an elite few.

Yet it was the more democratic Lummus brothers who made what is probably the most important and lasting early contribution to South Beach's enduring success. For it was J. E. and J. N. Lummus who created not only Ocean Drive but a beautiful three-quarter-mile-long park beside it, Lummus Park.

They spent more than $40,000 building and planting this park for the people, and they deeded it to the city in 1915 for only $40,000, payable over twenty years. It was certainly worth many times that even then. The brothers boasted that they hired the best lawyers in the county to make the deed ironclad, so that "Lummus Park will be a park always" and no residential or commercial structures could ever be built on it. (It was so ironclad that later, when J. N. Lummus had a momentary fit of regret and wanted the parkland back for a commercial project, he couldn't get it.) Some historians say the Lummuses were being less than purely altruistic when they sold the parkland to the city; and it is true they needed cash badly at the time and had sold a huge chunk of real estate west of Washington Avenue to Fisher for that reason. But they probably could have sold the beachfront land to Fisher, too, if all they cared about was the money. Instead, the Lummuses had the vision to see that an oceanfront park would make South Beach more successful. "A recreational park and bathing beach of sufficient area, extending along the ocean, was absolutely essential," wrote J. N. Lummus.

Proudly, in 1944, three decades after creating the park, J. N. Lummus declared: "Today the greatest asset Miami Beach has and will ever have is Lummus Park. It cannot be taken away from the public...It cannot be used for hotels or apartment houses. It belongs to the public for recreation and bathing."

Lummus Park today remains a delightfully green and open public space, an urban planning masterstroke that joins the city's finest boulevard, Ocean Drive, to the beach and ocean. Lummus was right, and the park's importance to South Beach's lasting appeal cannot be overstated. In a sense, the heart of South Beach is the beach, especially this famous beach that is part of the park. The ocean, the beach, then the greensward of the park, then the boulevard, the sidewalk cafés, the little hotels' veranda restaurants and interior lobbies: all form one, rich, unbroken, and vibrant continuum, filled with people.

Imagine how different Ocean Drive and all South Beach would be if developers could build high-rise hotels or apartment houses on what is now the park: soon the east side of Ocean Drive would be a nearly unbroken wall of concrete. Ocean views and beach access would be limited; and the high-rises (imagine the names: the Beach Club, Ocean View, or Park Tower) would cast long shadows, literally and figuratively, over the entire neighborhood. The high-rises would also jam more cars onto Ocean Drive, making it more polluted and less pedestrian-friendly.

Today Lummus Park remains a rare American example of private interests, developers, placing a huge chunk of the choicest land into the public realm — an act of enlightened self-interest so wise and farseeing that three-quarters of a century later this great public space, from the Atlantic to the very elevators in the public lobbies of the small hotels lining the western side of Ocean Drive, is one of the most beautiful, famous, and photogenic urban spaces in the world.

The beauty of this space attracts people; and the people make the space even more beautiful. Ocean Drive's international renown also derives from its being at once relaxed and exciting, having an unusually nice balance between man and nature, with its opening to the ocean and sky greeting the intimate but energetic buildings.

It's also worth looking at how the Lummus brothers developed their land (essentially everything south of Fifteenth Street), compared to how Fisher developed his (particularly his property north of Lincoln Road). "As early as 1915, a curious dichotomy" was evident between the Fisher and Lummus developments, writes historian Arlene Olson. In the Lummus lands "a predominantly proletariat atmosphere [with] ocean front rooming houses, lunch counters and bathing casinos" held sway: "A relaxed and hospitable atmosphere...open to anyone."

But in Fisher's territory, particularly in the mid-beach area where the dreadful condo-lined Concrete Canyon now stands, blocking off the ocean, Fisher "wanted his winter playground to cater to the rich and famous. The atmosphere he cultivated," Olson notes, "was restrictive and exclusive."

Carl Fisher thought big. He had made big money, and he built big hotels. He ballyhooed big highways to put all America on wheels. He sold big lots to big-shot industrialists who built big mansions. He owned big speedboats and held big boat races on Biscayne Bay, bringing in big names like carmaker Louis Chevrolet to pilot the noisy vessels. The only things Fisher seemed to like small were the bathing suits at the Miami Beach bathing beauty contests he staged. You want big: Fisher acquired two elephants (one named Carl) as enormous public relations gimmicks. Ever the showman, Fisher got pictures on page one of virtually every newspaper in America when he sent Rosie, one of his hulking Indian elephants, to caddie for President Warren G. Harding, with the pachyderm toting the chief executive's golf clubs around a big new Miami Beach hotel golf course that Fisher had built. Big, big, big. Yet for all his true greatness, Carl Fisher was also a sadly small-minded man. In Carl Fisher's hotels, in Carl Fisher's unwritten policy about exactly who could buy his properties, and throughout all of Carl Fisher's stupendous Miami Beach: No Jews allowed.

Schizophrenically, Fisher made quite a few exceptions when his expansive supersalesman's friendliness overwhelmed his narrow, provincial bigotry (especially when the Jews were "high class" in Fisher's mind), but basically Fisher's institutionalized anti-Semitism prevailed in much of Miami Beach north of Lincoln Road throughout the 1920s and 1930s. There were signs saying GENTILES ONLY, or even NO JEWS OR DOGS. Many hotels advertised with a code phrase: "Restricted clientele."

Despite the nastiness of it all, this attitude persisted until the late '40s, by which time the Nazi atrocities of World War II had made anti-Semitism no longer socially acceptable by anyone's stretch of the imagination.

"While Carl Fisher had his share of Jewish friends," a local Jewish magazine later wrote, "he felt it was good business to forbid his agents to sell plots or rent accommodations to them." Even Fisher's beaches were all private and "restricted," just like his hotels.

The Lummus brothers, on the other hand, thought small but were more open. Their lots were typically only fifty feet wide, and they'd do business regardless of religion. And instead of building enormous pleasure-dome hotels with private gardens, polo clubs, and "exclusive" private beaches, the Lummus Brothers built the crucial public park and beautiful public beach.

(Though some small hotels did so earlier, the first truly grand hotel on the Beach to welcome Jews was the Blackstone, which opened in 1929 in Lummus territory. One of its early guests was George Gershwin, and it is said he wrote parts of *Porgy and Bess* there. The fourteen-story Blackstone still stands, a handsomely renovated apartment house today, at 800 Washington Avenue.)

As for African-Americans, who had done so much of the backbreaking work of uprooting the jungle and planting the paradise, they generally weren't allowed anywhere on Miami Beach after 6:00 P.M. unless they had a written pass or resided in the servants' quarters of some wealthy white folk. For years Fisher employed a Negro manservant named Galloway as his butler and general factotum. But there were no black property owners in Carl Fisher's Miami Beach — or in the Lummuses', for that matter. They weren't welcome.

African-Americans, working as cooks, maids, waiters, porters, gardeners, or laborers, had to return from their jobs on the Beach to ramshackle ghettoes on the mainland; and in those days swimming was segregated throughout Florida, as were toilets,

schools, restaurants, and all other facilities.

At this point the mass-produced automobile, fast railroads, and post–World War I affluence were making Miami Beach more accessible to a fast-growing middle class. And to help bring them to Miami Beach, Fisher led a new crusade to convince governments to construct yet another paved road, this one running from Chicago to Florida. It was the Dixie Highway (also known as U.S. 1), and it delivered customers right to the door of Fisher's South Beach real estate office — and eventually to his hotels.

In appearance, Fisher resembled a slightly overstuffed, bald-headed teddy bear. He favored tweed sports jackets and large, white, broad-brimmed tropical planter hats. He was jolly and liked to fish and drink. Behind the big round glasses that he always wore, his eyes were shrewd and calculating.

On New Year's Eve, 1920–21, Fisher opened the Flamingo, Miami Beach's first truly grand hotel. On the bay near Lincoln Road at Fifteenth Street (where

Above: **New Year's Eve 1994–95 outside the Lizard Lounge of the Century Beach Club on Ocean Drive.** *Overleaf:* **The historic Blackstone, built in 1929, flanked by two newer buildings.**

there's now a sprawling high-rise apartment complex named Morton Towers), Carl Fisher's Flamingo was a sumptuous Moderne-style palace, eleven stories high and surmounted by a fabulous glass dome lit by multicolored spotlights and visible for miles, like some giant jewel. Pink flamingos, white herons, and black swans, all imported by Fisher, adorned the grounds. Fisher even installed a herd of cows, so his guests might have fresh milk each morning. At night, despite Prohibition, the booze and champagne flowed. Radiant at the private preopening party, Jane, then twenty-six years old, wore, the society column of the *Miami Herald* reported, "an exquisite Paris gown of blue lace over white satin with bodice drapery of blue embroidered with white. She wore a splendid string of pearls and a striking oriental headdress of dull red and orange-striped silk twisted cleverly into a turban," and long pendant earrings of tortoiseshell and gold. This was only eight years after an excited Fisher had dragged a reluctant young Jane through the swamps and drawn with a stick in the sand his plans for a great city. Now the city, the party, and the Flamingo were a sensation.

Its Gatsbyesque opening was the real start of the Roaring Twenties in South Beach and probably the ancestral beginnings of South Beach's present status as party central for much of the known universe.

The great Fisher, who slept with portraits of Napoleon and Lincoln over his bed (and with a brass spittoon to one side), continued his Miami Beach campaign by constructing a series of splendid hotels: the Lincoln, the Nautilus, the King Cole, the Floridian, and the Boulevard. (All are gone now, torn down, the last two over the objections of Barbara Capitman and the preservationists.)

"Now that Miami Beach was a success, it seemed everyone in the world came here," wrote Jane. "Women began wearing décolletage at dinner and the men formal attire." Movie stars, playwrights, concert artists, swimming champs, international polo players, statesmen, and tennis stars all flocked to Fisher's hotels to see and be seen. Sometimes Fisher discreetly paid the stars to come, to help build the resort's image.

Millionaires bought land from Fisher and built mansions there, men like J. C. Penney, R. J. Reynolds, Alfred Du Pont, and William Randolph Hearst. Their names read like a Who's Who of American business, many of them the founders of new, automobile-related fortunes, what some called Gasoline Society: Harvey Firestone (tires); Alfred Champion (spark plugs); C. F. Kettering (Delco and General Motors); Harry Stutz (Bearcat cars); Gar Wood (motor boats); John Hertz (taxis and rental cars); and Albert Lasker (advertising).

In 1920 Miami Beach's permanent population was only 644 people. Under Fisher, it grew tenfold in ten years. In 1930 the federal census counted 6,494 year-round residents. And that didn't count hotel guests and winter residents, who pushed the population during the Season (New Year's to Easter) much higher, to 30,000 by 1925, according to Fisher's enthusiastic figures. His former swamp was now a rich resort city.

"Night clubbing became the social outlet," wrote Jane. Singers, dancers, bandleaders, musicians, cabaret owners, and restaurateurs swept in from New York. A gold rush fever gripped everyone. Real estate speculation went wild throughout Florida, with salesmen citing the incredible transformation of Fisher's Miami Beach and the fortunes that could be yours in the Sunshine State, where it was June in January. Fueled by the Wall Street boom of the Roaring Twenties, buyers, investors, fortune seekers, and hucksters came by the thousands. Speculation based on buying property with a tiny "binder," or down payment, and then selling the real estate for much more, was like trading stock on margin in Wall Street. Sometimes the same piece of property, or rather paper, changed hands several times a day, and the prices kept going up.

Cars jammed the Dixie Highway, and it became so difficult to find a hotel room in the Miami area that bus stations were crowded with people living there. Other new arrivals simply slept in the streets of Miami Beach, or under the palms. One of those seeking his fortune was an out-of-work English newspaperman named T. H. Weigall. He stepped off the train in 1925 at the peak of the boom, and here's how he described the frenzied Miami he found:

> Hatless, coatless men rushed about the blazing streets, their arms full of papers, perspiration pouring from their foreheads. Every shop seemed to be combined with a real estate office…Everybody in Miami was real estate mad. Towering office buildings almost exclusively occupied by

realtors were scenes of incredible enthusiasm and confusion. Everywhere there was general handshaking, backslapping, and genial boasting. Everyone I saw seemed to be shaking hands, offering cigars and studying mysterious-looking diagrams of "desirable subdivisions."

And that was just his first day in town. That evening, drawn by the lights of one of Fisher's great hotels, Weigall, who was almost broke, walked across the bridge to Miami Beach.

"Considered purely as a pleasure resort, Miami Beach was at that time almost idyllic. Wide, golden beaches swept down to a crystal clear sea that was always warm; behind them palm groves and great sweeps of vivid green lawn stretched toward brilliantly white Spanish houses half-hidden behind hibiscus and magnolia trees," wrote Weigall, painting the picture-postcard Miami Beach of Carl Fisher, moonlit palms and all that. As he walked farther south, deeper into the Lummuses' less-manicured South Beach, the party atmosphere got hot.

Here's the party zone of the period, as described by historian Gloria Jahoda: "Down the streetcar line were the honky-tonks blaring 'Yessir, That's My Baby' and boop-boop-a-doop music, while cotton-clad flappers and their dates shook out Charlestons on postage stamp–sized dance floors and teenagers licked puffy towers of pink cotton candy." Jane Fisher called it an "all night long carnival…held under the well-advertised stars of Miami Beach," and that sums up South Beach nightlife rather well even now.

With Prohibition came speakeasies, bootleggers, and rum runners, the Florida coast perennially the perfect destination for smugglers in fast boats bringing in the stuff.

"From our windows we could see the flicker of the rum runners' lights out to sea," wrote Jane. "Huts mushroomed in the palmetto forests, and it became smart to drive around at midnight to these palm-thatched dens to gamble and drink bad liquor sold at exorbitant rates." Later, a dog track was built in South Pointe and a pier with a burlesque house on it, featuring Minsky's finest strippers.

Also rushing into Miami Beach were "the gold-diggers and the sugar-daddies, the gigolos…the play-boys, and the gilded heiresses, the professional huntresses," wrote Jane bitterly. Her marriage was collapsing. Carl enjoyed numerous quick affairs, plus a long-term one with his secretary. Jane took long, lavish trips to Egypt and Paris, where she took a young lover who tried to blackmail her. The Fishers eventually divorced in 1926, and Carl sold their beautiful South Beach mansion. Named the Shadows, it stood at the end of Lincoln Road overlooking the beach and had been the brilliant epicenter of South Beach society.

The Shadows is gone now, replaced by an enormous condominium apartment house called the Decoplage. But a few of Carl Fisher's buildings remain, among them the Lincoln Building, built in 1924 as Fisher's office (restored seventy years later as the Van Dyke Hotel and Café) in the 800 block of Lincoln Road; and the Spanish Mission–style Miami Beach Community Church at 500 Lincoln Road, built by Fisher in 1921 after Jane insisted the city needed a church.

The real estate bubble was still expanding when a huge hurricane hit in 1926. The winds hit 128 miles an hour before they blew the weather instruments away. Then the storm surge, a sort of tidal wave, crashed across Miami Beach, depositing two to four feet of sand and thousands of fish everywhere, including the hotel lobbies. One of Fisher's real estate salesmen survived the surge by hanging on to an office chandelier. Some wooden buildings were pulled off their foundations and wrecked. The storm killed nearly 400 people in the Miami area, injured 6,000, and left some 25,000 homeless, ending the Florida land rush, bursting the real estate bubble, and tossing the region's economy into a tailspin. Many property owners could no longer afford to pay their mortgages or meet their margin calls. Within a year, dozens of Florida banks went belly-up.

Next, an even bigger disaster blew in: the Wall Street crash of 1929. The whole world's boom went bust. Fisher, overextended in Miami Beach and in an elaborate Montauk, New York, luxury community he was building, lost $25 million and most of his properties in the ensuing crisis, became a drunkard, and eventually, in 1935, declared personal bankruptcy. As for Jane, she had a series of costly marriages to younger men. Yet she and Carl loyally stayed best friends, though both remarried. Carl died almost in obscurity in Miami Beach in 1939, leaving a paltry $50,000 estate. After his death, Jane burnished his reputation by writing her vivid memoirs about the early days. Eventually she too lost most of her money and property, though she always remained a good interview for journalists and historians. She died in Miami Beach in 1969.

But the legacy of the pioneers lived on. The town the Fishers and the Lummus brothers created set the pattern for today's South Beach. It is still an American Riviera, blessed with gorgeous winter weather and a superb geographic location. And it is still oscillating schizophrenically between the uptown, nouveau-riche, big-money snootiness of the flamboyant Fishers with their grandiose, internationally attended parties and the populist, downtown, dance-club, bathing-casino, public-park, party-zone democracy of the farsighted Lummus brothers. In fact, it's the collision and the marriage of these two contrasting South Beach cultures that make the place so dynamic.

North of Lincoln Road remains relatively staid, with generally larger lots, larger hotels, and larger private homes. And south of Lincoln Road is still where most of the beachfront fun, neon, and nightclubs are. The Lummus-platted lots are still small, creating a wealth of small buildings and a generally more affordable, though still very nice, ambience.

Illegal substances and vice, which jumped into Miami Beach in a big way during the Roaring Twenties, still spice up the town for better or for worse. The seasonal threat of a major hurricane still adds an air of impermanence to life in a pleasure dome built on a sandbar. And a certain Fisheresque flamboyance in the public relations sphere and in

architecture still makes South Beach glow like a beacon, visible from afar like the floodlit crystal summit of the long-gone Flamingo Hotel.

Yet, for all its glamorous nightlife, South Beach was, and still remains, a delightful residential neighborhood, though in its early years it was far more idyllic than today. Recently, interior designer Edith Irma Siegel recalled the gardenlike quality of life in South Beach of 1930, when she had a little winter cottage at Drexel and Fifteenth: "It was quiet and beautiful and clean, and the flowers were gorgeous and the jasmine. I'll never forget waking up to the scent of jasmine. And all the birds on the windowsills. It was so unsullied…there weren't many buildings, you know, past Seventeenth Street."

It was into this fertile South Beach of the 1930s that a new and elegant form of architecture was imported. From Paris, Hollywood, and New York, Art Deco was transplanted into South Beach's sandy soil. There, baked by the sun and drenched by the rain, it would take root, grow, mutate, and splendidly flower, becoming an exotic yet hardy new species — Tropical Deco.

Above: **Modern new shapes sprang up in subtropical South Beach, including this streamlined building by Dixon from about 1940.** *Opposite:* **The Raleigh Hotel pool by Dixon. In the late 1940s** *Life* **magazine called it the most beautiful pool in Florida. Some say it still is.**

Above and right: **A Hohauser building, 444 Ocean Drive, photographed a few years apart. Advocates say the newer, brighte[r] purists maintain these buildings should be painted almost all white, as they were in th[e]**

DECO FOREVER

"The surest test of the civilization of a people — at least, as sure a test as any...is to be found in their architecture, which presents so noble a field for the display of the grand and the beautiful, and which, at the same time, is so intimately connected with the essential comforts of life." — *William Hickling Prescott in* The Conquest of Peru

Most of South Beach, hundreds of Art Deco buildings, sprang up in only eight years: 1934 through 1941. This great flowering of architectural creativity was rapid, even by the tropical hothouse standards of Florida, where feverish real estate booms and busts came in cycles as natural as the sunshine and rain. And South Beach was no quickie tract development with hundreds of identical and uninspired buildings. In South Beach each building was one-of-a-kind; and the over-all artistic quality was high.

A half-dozen architects had almost spontaneously created South Beach's signature style: Tropical Deco. It is this style (albeit with considerable individuality and diversity within it) that gives South Beach its remarkably consistent and exotic look. Many of the buildings were masterpieces. Almost all show verve, charm, and imagination. The Tropical Deco buildings were casually elegant, but they were not costly; they were made of

colors make the Deco details more visible. But some 1930s and 1940s.

common materials like reinforced concrete. Yet taken together, these six or seven hundred intimately scaled and inexpensive buildings wove an urban fabric so beautiful and comfortable that it has enchanted three or four generations already; and thanks to the preservationists, it now seems likely, if greed and bad planning don't ruin it, that South Beach's historic district will survive for centuries as one of the world's loveliest and most livable city neighborhoods.

Like other celebrated centers — the old city of Florence; the charming district around Amsterdam's central canals; or the old temple-palace-market city of Kathmandu in the Himalayan kingdom of Nepal — South Beach is not only an architectural achievement, but is also a mecca for tourism, shopping, and commerce. And for all their obvious differences, these far-flung examples bear remarkable similiarities: they are all old-fashioned, low-rise, pedestrian-oriented neighborhoods with a vibrant street life, a strong artistic flavor, and a uniquely local character. But, compared to the creation of a city like Florence, which evolved over centuries, what happened in South Beach was explosively fast.

A few of South Beach's wonderful Tropical Deco buildings were built as early as 1930; and a few wonderful ones came considerably later (from 1945 to about 1950). But the heart of the Tropical Deco period, eight years — 1934 through 1941 — coincides with the Swing Era and the beginning of modern aviation.

It is a Flash Gordon age of technological revolutions: time and space are telescoped by new means of communication and transportation. Radio and Hollywood reign worldwide. Ocean liners are swifter, sleeker, and more luxurious than ever; and the new long-range passenger planes — particularly Pan American's high-winged Sikorski S-42 Clippers (huge, four-engined "flying boats" to Bermuda, San Juan, Havana, and Rio de Janeiro) and Eastern Airlines' "Great Silver Fleet" of streamlined, state-of-the-art DC-3s capable of hopscotching to New York at nearly 180 miles per hour — make Miami a major hub. Even the sky is no limit. Rocket ships, other planets, and futuristic cities are widely imagined and illustrated in popular magazines, comic strips, and movies.

All this profoundly affects the architecture and ambience of Miami Beach as the American Riviera. The '20s are finished: Fisher's era of flivvers, flappers, and pseudo-aristocratic Mediterranean Revival–style palaces is past. The '30s will be a Modern Age.

It's in this context that Tropical Deco takes off in 1934 (despite the Great Depression) and soars ahead with an astonishing display of visual brilliance until the Japanese attack on Pearl Harbor in 1941 suddenly ends the construction boom and throws Miami Beach into the war effort, with the U.S. Army commandeering most of the hotels and turning the island into an Air Corps training camp for the duration. But South Beach's eight-year Deco boom had been spectacular.

One of the greatest Tropical Deco architects was L. Murray Dixon. He designed the Marlin Hotel and hundreds of other Deco structures, including the Raleigh Hotel and its sensational swimming pool, plus the Victor, Ocean Front, Tides, Imperial, and McAlpin hotels on Ocean Drive. His output was staggering: Dixon designed 42 hotels, 87 apartment buildings, 33 store buildings, 220 private homes, 2 housing developments, 31 building renovations, and

16 miscellaneous buildings: 431 projects in all, most in the Tropical Deco style and in South Beach, and all in only eighteen years — that's about two buildings a month!

Unlike most architects today (but like most of his Tropical Deco peers), Dixon designed not only a building's basic plan but nearly every important detail: the decorative bas-reliefs, the light fixtures, the terrazzo floors, the ornamental screen doors, and the entire lobby of his hotels, even the furniture.

Dixon was only forty-eight years old when he died of a cerebral hemor-rhage in 1949. But his son, L. Murray Dixon Jr., also an architect, remembers well the frenetic excite-ment of the Deco boom, for he worked summers as his father's apprentice. "It was an awful lot of fun," said Dixon Jr. Work was so abundant that all the archi-tects were incredibly busy, so there was little of the usual professional rivalry for commissions. But friendly competition on an artistic level heated up among these architects, like jazz musicians in some epic jam session. "Say you happen to be in a city that creates great music," explained Dixon Jr. "Like New Orleans in the days of Louis Armstrong and King Oliver. One musician excites the others and then — it happens…It was a lot of talent, a lot of interplay…

"Just like members of a band create little riffs," said Dixon — referring to the catchy rhythmic and melodic motifs that are structural and decorative

elements in jazz — the Tropical Deco group created visual riffs that they tossed around and played with, each architect improvising heroic solo variations before the whole group would come back in and repeat the virtually rhythmic visual riffs together. This is the way numerous South Beach buildings by many different architects were unified: by repeated motifs. And, according to architectural draftsman S. Arthur Pepp, who knew them all, after work many of the architects, including Dixon, Roy F. France, and Igor Polevitsky, could be found "drinking lustily" together at a bar called the Royal Palm Club.

During the day, they shared an enormous feel-ing of excitement. "Every-one looked forward to coming to work," recalls Dixon Jr. The architects knew they were creating something special. They worked at a tremendous pace. Dixon Jr. remembers construction schedules so tight that "I was pushing wheelbarrows of concrete up ramps at night with lights on and everyone was going crazy because the building had to be open when the Season opened."

Wrote *Architectural Forum* magazine in December 1940: "Chatter of riveting machines com-petes with the roll of the surf along Miami Beach. Looming just ahead is December 16, at which time the chatter must stop…Officially, according to city ordinance, the tourist season opens and the city's guests must be allowed to sleep in peace. Meanwhile, forty-one new hotels are being rushed to completion."

Among them were the Raleigh and the Ritz-Plaza (both by Dixon), the National (by France), and the astonishingly clean-lined and advanced-looking Shelborne (by the Russian-born Polevitsky) — and these four hotels by the three friends are all on a one-and-a-half-block stretch of Collins Avenue.

Opposite: **Flash Gordon modern on Euclid Avenue — an L. Murray Dixon apartment building, built circa 1940, framed by another by Roy F. France, built in 1937.** *Above:* **The Shelborne by Igor Polevitsky, also built in 1940.**

South Beach's Deco boom was at its peak, and it was even bigger than the great boom of 1925. Back in 1925, in the wake of Fisher's Flamingo, 21 hotels and 101 apartment buildings had gone up in Miami

Beach. In 1941, however, a record 41 hotels and 166 apartment buildings were constructed. Hitler's war in Europe was helping fuel the boom, as much international investment capital sought a safe haven in Miami Beach, *Architectural Forum* reported.

Even the superprolific Dixon couldn't design his buildings alone; he had a

staff of some six draftsmen. And by no means are all of his buildings masterpieces, though all are interesting. Many, especially his ubiquitous two-story apartment houses, seem variations of the same design, but no two are identical, and these variations on a theme, scattered about the district, add to the fascination of the place. Walking around, you begin recognizing the resemblances among the Deco buildings, almost as if each were an individual member of the same family. These family resemblances go further than just Dixon's designs; a stylistic kinship unites virtually all the architects working in the district then. This is particularly noticeable in two instances, when Dixon designed wonderful buildings next to masterpieces

Opposite: **The Colony.** *Above left:* **Workers install neon on the Crescent.** *Above right:* **It's on!** *Center:* **The Park Central (at left) and the Imperial (at right) seem as one.** *Overleaf:* **The Crescent and McAlpin.**

by the great Henry Hohauser.

Hohauser was second only to Dixon in quantity of Tropical Deco buildings, but in quality Hohauser probably surpasses Dixon, if only for consistency.

While the prolific Dixon's genius was a bit uneven, virtually every building Hohauser drew was elegant and exciting.

Hohauser's finest include the Century at 140 Ocean Drive (1939); the Surf at 444 Ocean Drive (1936); the Colony (probably the most photographed building in South Beach, beloved by fashion photographers and tourists alike) at 736 Ocean Drive (1935); and the Park Central at 630 Ocean Drive (1937).

Two years after Hohauser designed the beautiful Park Central, his friend Dixon was commissioned to design a small hotel, the Imperial, next door. They fit together perfectly, though the Park Central is seven stories and the Imperial only three. Dixon's Imperial was just another variation on one of his favorite plans, but in elegance and verve, it's one of his best. Highlighting the unity of the two buildings is an elegant and subtle color scheme that the late Leonard Horowitz gave both buildings and which their present owner, South Beach and SoHo real estate mogul, hotelier, and sometime jazz singer Tony Goldman, maintains beautifully.

Another witty Hohauser-Dixon double feature is the Crescent at 1420 Ocean Drive (Hohauser, 1938) and the McAlpin next door (Dixon, 1940). Both buildings are three stories, and their lines,

particularly the streamlined "eyebrows" over their windows, unite them.

Cantilevered concrete "eyebrows," or sunshades, are a big part of the city's signature look. You see them on perhaps half the Tropical Deco buildings in South Beach. Nowhere else in the world are these Deco sunshades so typical, though examples can be found on some Deco buildings in such sunny climes as Southern California, India, Morocco, and Puerto Rico.

Deco was an astonishingly universal style, popping up in locations as remote as Pakistan and Indonesia, not to mention all over the United States, Europe, South America, Australia, and New Zealand. Scholarly conferences called the World Congress on Art Deco, begun by Barbara Capitman and continued by her friend Michael Kinerk and others in the United States and abroad, are still exploring the history of how all this happened, but it is clear that Deco was a worldwide design movement, spread partly by a series of world fairs and international expositions in the 1920s and 1930s, and by movies and photographs. And though South Beach is usually considered the world capital of Tropical Deco, it appears that Tropical Deco, or something very much like it, sprang up in several other coastal cities, said Kinerk, most notably Perth, Australia, and Napier, New Zealand.

But to understand Tropical Deco in South Beach, it helps to look at its predecessor in Florida: Mediterranean Revival.

At first glance, Art Deco may seem a bold, modernist reaction against the ornate and nostalgic Mediterranean Revival style. But a closer look also shows underlying similarities. Before Art Deco, Mediterranean Revival was Florida's signature style. Classic hotels constructed by Flagler and Fisher (and the mansions erected by their millionaire friends) were almost invariably in this grand style. Mediterranean Revival was, despite its name, more native to Florida and California than to the Mediterranean. It was a glorious American mishmash of Spanish, Italian, French, and Moorish motifs: a fairy-tale architecture of romantic balconies, red tile roofs, arched colonnades, decorative carvings, tiled fountains, ornate metal gates, soaring bell towers, and glowing white, gold, or rose-colored walls of stucco festooned with ornamentation: heraldic medallions, friezes, statues, and finials. Against Florida's sunny blue skies and white cottonball clouds, these huge castles were wonderfully picturesque.

It was Beaux Arts meets Spanish Colonial, a neotraditional look that invoked Florida's Spanish heritage and imparted a romantic feeling of long, perhaps even aristocratic, lineage to what was essentially a new, swampy, and until very recently mostly mosquito-infested wilderness. At its best, Mediterranean Revival, with its graceful gardens, cool fountains, shady courtyards, arched colonnades, and artful decoration, was delightful and well-suited to Florida's often sweltering subtropical weather. At its worst, the style was ponderous and pretentious with all its baronial trappings.

The Mediterranean Revival style was soon applied to everything, not just to grand hotels, country clubs, and mansions. The 1920s in Florida were filled with Mediterranean Revival office buildings, churches, schools, fire stations, and smaller private homes, even some charming bungalows. There were other Florida styles, of course, including wood-frame homes built on the Bahamian or Key West model, but what really symbolized early twentieth-century Florida, with all its flamboyant excesses and tropical allure, was Mediterranean Revival.

South Beach retains many fine examples, including dozens of charming, small apartment houses built just before the Deco era and recently restored along with their Deco neighbors to great effect.

But the most enduringly popular Mediterranean Revival work in South Beach is an eight-building Spanish fantasy extravaganza, originally named "the Spanish Village," constructed in 1925 by developer N. B. T. Roney on two blocks of a street named Espanola Way. There are balconies galore, arches, red tile roofs, small hotels, sidewalk cafés, nightclubs, boutiques, and artists' studios there now. Roney intended this to be an artists' colony, a sort of subtropical Greenwich Village, but it soon became a red light district, with fashionable brothels and nightclubs. There, in the 1930s, a young Cuban exile bandleader named Desiderio Alberto Arnaz III — Desi

Opposite: **Full Mediterranean Revival with everything — a balcony supported by spiral fluted columns, pink stucco walls adorned with a heraldic medallion, Assyrian mythical beasts on the bas-reliefs, and a Spanish mission–style pediment on top.**

Arnaz — taught America to rumba.

Today, these two blocks of Espanola Way look much as they did in 1925, except that the original window frames, which opened like doors from hinges on one side, have been replaced, in some cases with sleek Deco-style aluminum frame windows with wide, horizontal louvers, lending the Mediterranean Revival architecture a more streamlined look. Actually, there was already a certain playful, cartoonlike simplicity and abstraction in architect Robert Taylor's 1925 rendering of Mediterranean Revival on Espanola Way, a hint of a coming modernist revolution.

Revolutions in technology, economics, and politics were already upsetting the established social order throughout the industrialized world, and from the chaos emerged new styles. Art Nouveau was an attempt in the 1890s to bridge the "romantic traditionalism of nineteenth-century Victorian society with the new products of the industrial revolution. [But] Art Nouveau raised more questions than it answered," writes Ivan A. Rodriguez, describing the trends leading to Tropical Deco.

The "sinuous, soft organic curves" and natural motifs of Art Nouveau were beautiful, but incongruous in a brutally mechanized age: "World War I jolted the arts from its last vestige of complacent traditionalism," continues Rodriguez. "Forms were stripped to bare bones, their structures re-examined and the components arranged in statements of new architectural honesty...the radical, the avant garde, the abstract replace historicism," says Rodriguez in the excellent book, *From Wilderness to Metropolis: The History and Architecture of Dade County, Florida (1825–1940),* published by the county's Historic Preservation Division.

The German Bauhaus, the Dutch De Stijl, and the Russian Constructivism, "all had the same back-to-basics simplicity in their architectural vocabulary," observes Rodriguez. "Roofs were flat, surfaces were finished in smooth, white stucco, glass, and metal."

Showing an abstraction akin to Cubism, this was a truly modern architecture and would eventually be named the International Style. But, continues Rodriguez, "the new architectural austerity left many

Above, opposite, and previous spread: **Espanola Way — Taylor and Roney's Spanish fantasy.**

admirers and practitioners of the old design schools unimpressed."

Then, in the 1920s, the two opposing styles — the lush ornamentation of the traditionalists and the stark geometry of the modernists — were combined into a dramatic new style. Giving the synthesis a certain exoticism were novel geometric and natural motifs inspired by ancient civilizations, notably the Mayan, Babylonian, and Egyptian. (In 1922 a British archaeologist had discovered and opened King Tut's stunningly decorated tomb, touching off an Egyptian vogue.) Mix all together, and — voilà —you had Art Deco.

The new style was launched in Paris in 1925 at the Exposition Internationale des Arts Décoratifs et Industriels Modernes, a spectacular world's fair of architecture and design featuring pavilions of tremendous beauty and imagination erected on both banks of the Seine in the heart of Paris. Some twenty nations built pavilions to showcase their designers and their wares: modern furniture, textiles, glassware, model homes, and the like. Pavilions were also erected by the city of Paris and by several great Parisian department stores. Individual manufacturers

and entire industries also sponsored grand pavilions. There were 120 pavilions in all, most displaying the exhilarating new Art Deco style. The exposition opened in April, and before it closed in October, nearly six million people from around the world had come to the fair.

The United States had been invited to build a national pavilion. But Secretary of Commerce Herbert Hoover declined, saying the United States was not yet able to meet the exposition's requirement that everything be of modern design. Hoover did, however, send a large delegation of American designers and manufacturers to study the chic modern styles on display. Naturally, the Paris show also attracted many other American visitors. Not least was a handsome young native New Yorker named Cedric Gibbons, who had worked briefly as a draftsman in his father's architectural firm before joining the world's largest movie studio, Metro-Goldwyn-Mayer, in 1924 as its supervising art director.

Deco's conquest of the design world was far too sweeping to be the work of any one person; yet it's probably not too much to say that more than anyone

else in the world it was Cedric Gibbons who introduced the great American public to Art Deco — and, in the late 1920s and early 1930s, made the style synonymous with glamour.

Gibbons himself was movie-star glamorous. He looked, dressed, and behaved like a suave matinee idol. He drove a fast white Duesenberg roadster and married the exquisite Mexican-born RKO movie star

statuette, a sleek Art Deco figurine. That was in 1928, and he went on in a four-decade-long career to win a full dozen Oscars himself. And it was Gibbons, the great Gibbons, who made Art Deco MGM's — and America's — new high style.

The sensational 1928 Joan Crawford hit, *Our Dancing Daughter*, while not the first film to showcase the styles of the Paris Exposition, was the first to

Dolores Del Rio (who danced with Astaire in *Flying Down to Rio* in 1932). Gibbons and his exotic wife lived in a streamlined white Art Deco, Gibbons-designed Santa Monica Canyon home, where they held lavish, star-studded parties (and where the greatest of all Hollywood glamour photographers, George Hurrell, would photograph Del Rio and her designer husband). You can't get more Hollywood than this: Gibbons designed that most sacred totem of movieland glamour, the Academy Awards' Oscar

Opposite: **More literal, decorative, classical design typifies earlier Tropical Deco.** *Above:* **More abstract, geometric, and streamlined design typical of later Tropical Deco.**

make Deco fashionable in America. After the movie, American department stores began carrying Art Deco furnishings similar to those in the film. Under Gibbons's supervision, this film's Deco sets were by the young Richard Day (who later designed such disparate classics as *The Grapes of Wrath* and *A Streetcar Named Desire*). Meanwhile, dozens of other MGM films designed under Gibbons's supervision, most notably *Grand Hotel* (1932) with Garbo and Crawford, established Art Deco in the American public's mind as the sumptuous, cosmopolitan, modern style that one would naturally expect to find in the most fashionable hotels in the world.

Hollywood made Deco big. RKO's Fred Astaire and Ginger Rogers movies featured tremendous

Deco and Streamline Moderne sets, again in the context of showing how the rich supposedly lived, in grand hotels, luxurious ocean liners, and fantastic nightclubs. MGM may have set the trend, but in the Hollywood films of the 1930s all the studios created extravagant Deco interiors, especially in scenes portraying lavish nightclubs, deluxe travel, fashionable hotels, and the stylishly appointed apartments of rich and desirable entertainment stars, smooth-as-silk gangsters, and beautiful kept women. In the 1930s Hollywood formula, Art Deco equaled smart, racy glamour.

There's a life-imitating-art-imitating-life dizziness to the popularization of Art Deco in America. Some MGM stars actually had Gibbons design the interior of their homes as exact replicas of the stylish Deco movie sets he had designed for them to act in. Other fabulously wealthy people also beseeched Gibbons to design their real homes in the style to which they had become accustomed — in his movies.

All this played back in South Beach only a few years later, when a new wave of fairly sophisticated entrepreneurs, many of them successful Jewish small businessmen from New York and some Italian and Jewish gangsters from Chicago and New York, commissioned architects like Dixon and Hohauser to build, in the heart of the Depression, a series of carefree Miami Beach vacation hotels and chic nightclub-casinos that would convey the glamour, excitement, and style of the era's high life.

From the very beginning Florida had been a land of fantasy. Pioneer developers, including the great Flagler and Fisher, sold romantic visions of an old-regime grandeur in the form of sprawling pseudo-European palaces. Although Mediterranean Revival has never gone completely out of style and still retains a certain cachet in Florida, by 1930 the smart young set wanted Art Deco.

Meanwhile, the dialectic between lush, old-style ornamentation and stark new Machine Age simplicity, the very tension that had created Art Deco, was never completely resolved.

During the '20s, '30s, and '40s a swarm of somewhat related styles with revealing names like Zig-Zag Moderne, Streamline Moderne, and Futurism emerged. Zig-Zag leaned to the decorative, absorbing motifs from Mayan pyramids and Babylonian ziggurats. It's associated with some New York skyscrapers, Los Angeles Art Deco, and a Southwestern American style of architecture called Pueblo Deco that drew from local American Indian motifs.

Streamline Moderne, as the name implies, was more of a pure Machine Age modernism, taking its design cues from the sleekly rounded, aerodynamic shape of aircraft, fast cars, and luxury liners. There were all sorts of other regional or function-based styles and substyles, including Depression Moderne, a form typically found on massive government or corporate buildings that mixed classical elements with fairly stark streamlining. (A good example is South Beach's main post office at 1300 Washington Avenue.)

In theory, early, pure Deco has more decoration than pure Moderne (which like the International Style is rectilinearly geometric) or Streamline Moderne, which added sensuous curves to the International Style's right angles.

Opposite: **Depression Modern — the gym of the Ida M. Fisher Junior High School, designed by August Geiger in 1936 and funded by New Deal President Franklin D. Roosevelt's far-reaching Public Works Administration.** *Above:* **South Beach's main post office, designed by Howard L. Chesney in 1937 and built by another of FDR's agencies, the Works Progress Administration, which hired not only skilled artisans but also unskilled workers and trained them on the job.**

But all these pedantic terms can get confusing. At least one architectural historian insists that South Beach's world-renowned Art Deco District was fundamentally misnamed and really ought to be renamed the Streamline Moderne District, but that's silly. It certainly loses the alliteration of the Art Deco District, and it just doesn't have the same ring to it. But it is true that no one called these buildings Art Deco at the time they were built.

The term didn't even exist (at least not in English) until 1966, when historian Bevis Hillier, writing a catalog for a museum retrospective on the great 1925 Paris exposition, coined the phrase "Art Deco" (a contraction of the words *Arts Décoratifs* in the great exposition's name). In any event, "Art Deco" caught on almost overnight as an umbrella term for an entire design era, including all its sub- and related styles. "Art Deco" was short, sweet, and evocative: heaven-sent for headline writers, journalists, and preservation proselytizers like Barbara Capitman, who personally did much to popularize the term.

What's more, the scholarly distinctions between early, supposedly more ornamented Art Deco and the later, supposedly more stark

Opposite: **This classic American streamlined stainless steel diner was built in 1948 by the Paramount Dining Car Co. in New Jersey, and served traditional American food for forty-four years in Wilkes Barre, Pennsylvania, until 1992 when three young entrepreneurs moved it to South Beach, where it became a success as the Eleventh Street Diner. Our waitress is Christina Lyons.**

Streamline Moderne break down even more than usual in South Beach — where applied decoration (often friezes or sculpted panels depicting Florida motifs like fountains, fish, or flamingos, or sometimes just abstract geometric forms) blossom in tropical profusion on the walls of many of the most streamlined South Beach buildings. Like Mediterranean Revival, Tropical Deco is a gloriously eclectic mishmash of styles.

Hohauser and Dixon even designed some buildings that mixed Art Deco or Streamline techniques with traditional Mediterranean Revival motifs: red tile roofs, balconies, plaster medallions on the walls, the works. The decorative impulse is very strong in Florida, and the Tropical Deco masters decorated even humble screen doors with exuberant designs: sunbeams and palm trees, flamingos and seascapes — pure Floridiana.

Again like Mediterranean Revival, Tropical Deco is a whimsical architecture, full of fantasy and fun. Like a Hollywood set, part of its job was to entertain and enchant. Some say this was a resort town reaction against the grim Depression of the 1930s, and it was, but a whimsical fantasy quality runs through much Florida architecture from Flagler to Disney. Perhaps this stage-set quality is why South Beach works so well as the backdrop for TV shows, fashion spreads, and the almost theatrically exhibitionistic subcultures of the drag queens, the Rollerbladers, the bodybuilders, and the fashion models.

There's also a futuristic, technologically advanced aspect to Tropical Deco. Solar hot-water systems were originally built into many small Tropical Deco apartment

rative horizontal lines to objects, including buildings, to give them dynamism and motion, like the streaking lines in a cartoon portraying speed. These streamlines were added to the ultra-modern designs of such disparate 1930s objects as railroad locomotives, automobiles, vacuum cleaners, kitchen appliances, and South Beach buildings. The teardrop shape of airfoils (airplane wings), fast cars, and boats was also part of the streamline aesthetic. But futurism went yet further into fantasy, invoking a look not merely of airplanes or fast trains — but of rocket ships and imagined twenty-first-century cities.

Some writers have dubbed this part of the South Beach style Buck Rogers Deco, after the comic strip spaceman created in 1929 — but this just misses the mark. The drawing in the *Buck Rogers* strip was clunky and stiff. Far more elegant, sexy, and supple, was *Flash Gordon,* created, written, and drawn by Alex Raymond beginning in 1934, coincident with the launch of the Tropical Deco period. An exquisitely styled and instantly popular fantasy, which featured scantily clad heroes and heroines, villains

houses and private residences back in the 1930s! Solar still makes economic sense in the Sunshine State, but unfortunately solar systems on the older buildings generally have not been maintained, and most buildings constructed in Florida today totally lack solar, depending on dirtier and costlier fossil fuels to heat water.

On a more purely decorative level, a futurism based on notions of scientific progress and science fiction adventure expressed itself in the soaring pylons and fins on many Tropical Deco buildings — reminiscent of the style of the New York World's Fair of 1939 with its "Building the World of Tomorrow" theme, its "Rocketport of the Future" exhibit designed by Raymond Loewy for the Chrysler Corporation, and the even more popular and influential exhibit by Norman Bel Geddes in the General Motors pavilion. Called "Futurama," it featured huge models of soaring cities and superhighways: a vision of the world of far-off 1960.

The streamline style of the 1930s, based loosely on notions of aerodynamics and speed, added deco-

and the Tiffany (both erected in the World's Fair year of 1939), resembled something Flash might encounter in one of his Sunday panels.

The *Flash Gordon*–South Beach affinities are only deepened by the fantastic Deco sets and flamboyant costumes in three hugely popular blockbuster movie serials made by Universal Studios, starring Olympic swimming hero Buster Crabbe: *Flash Gordon* (1936), *Flash Gordon's Trip to Mars* (1938), and *Flash Gordon Conquers the Universe* (1940), which together fit neatly into the Tropical Deco time in which a futuristic architecture from outer space conquered, if not the universe, at least parts of Planet South Beach.

Somewhat closer to earth, the Tropical Deco architects also indulged nautical fantasies: many buildings drew their inspiration from luxury liners. The buildings' porthole windows, sleek pipe railings, fins, flagstaffs, masts, and sleekly rounded walls all call to mind the towering, curved hulls, elegant upper decks, and streamlined superstructures of the great oceangoing liners. Excellent examples are the Beach

and vixens, as well as great rocket ships and soaring futuristic cities, *Flash Gordon* was much more in step with South Beach — even the otherworldly South Beach of today, where certain leading club personalities resemble the strip's unforgettable villain, the Emperor Ming of Planet Mongo (complete with shaved head, goatee beard, and heavy-duty jewelry), and where curvy club kittens dress in slave-girl chic like Ming's beautiful daughter, the slinky Princess Aura, or Flash's ever-faithful sweetheart, Dale Arden (who kept finding herself chained and whipped by both men and women in the comic strip, not unlike some girls in South Beach S&M nightclub extravaganzas today). Also, the towers and antennae that Dixon added to some of his hotels, notably the Kent

CALLING FLASH GORDON! *From left, opposite:* **The Adams Hotel, 1938, the Kent Hotel, 1939, the Tiffany Hotel, 1939 (all by Dixon); and a circa 1936 light fixture in the former French Casino, now Glam Slam, a nightclub owned by the artist formerly known as Prince.**

Patrol Headquarters on the oceanfront at Lummus Park and Tenth Street and the Albion Hotel (Polevitsky, 1939) on Lincoln Road. But maybe the most poignant example of Nautical Moderne is Hohauser's Greystone Hotel (1939). It's often said that great ocean liners and cruise ships are like floating hotels. But the Greystone is a resort hotel like a landlocked ship, ready to sail but stuck forever on its corner at Collins and Twentieth.

Another inspiration, particularly for the taller Tropical Deco buildings, were the romantic skyscrapers of Manhattan. Both Dixon and Hohauser began their careers in New York during the late 1920s and early 1930s, just as the Art Deco skyscraper era there reached its spectacular peak. Dixon was a project manager at Schultze and Weaver, the firm that designed New York's quintessential Art Deco hotel, the Waldorf-Astoria, in 1931 (faint echoes of which can be found in Dixon's Ritz-Plaza of 1940 at Collins Avenue and Seventeenth). Also at Schultze and Weaver at the time was Edward Durrell Stone, who would go on to design the Museum of Modern Art, and whose desk was next to Dixon's.

Meanwhile, Hohauser, a native New Yorker, was working in the large New York firm of his cousin William Hohauser and was greatly influenced by the Forty-second Street skyscrapers, especially the now-often-overlooked Chanin Building, a 1929 Art Deco masterpiece, which was briefly the tallest building in the world and which features lush decorative friezes that inspired several South Beach architects.

No expense was spared in ornamenting Manhattan's world-beating Deco skyscrapers. Materials were opulent: marble lobbies; elevators inlaid with rare tropical woods; and countless ornamental details in exquisitely wrought, engraved, sculpted, and burnished metals. By contrast, the far more modest Tropical Deco buildings of South Beach were built on a much smaller budget, and the materials were far more humble. Instead of marble, there might be floors of Florida terrazzo (colored stone chips set in mortar and polished when dry) or walls partially clad in keystone (a highly porous stone from the Florida Keys that could be dyed different colors). The basic construction was usually simple: reinforced-concrete floors and columns, with concrete-block exterior walls, stuccoed over and then painted. Many small Tropical Deco buildings were essentially concrete boxes.

What made them great was the sensitive massing of their facades, the graceful decorative lines, and the superb ornamentation the architects gave them, drawing equally from the high Deco heritage of the New York school and from the Mediterranean Revival artisan tradition of old Florida. Some of the finest Tropical Deco buildings also have a sensuous sculptural feel.

In addition to Dixon and Hohauser, the other great Tropical Deco architects in South Beach include the Russian-born Igor Polevitsky; Anton Skislewicz, born in the picturesque coastal city of Dubrovnik in the former Yugoslavia; Albert Anis from Chicago; and Roy F. France from Minnesota.

Together, with perhaps a few others who were not as prolific, these half-dozen architects gave South Beach its relaxed, elegant, whimsical, futuristic, yet humanistic style: Tropical Deco, a classic modernism that seems today at once old-fashioned and avant-garde, and is still a pleasure to live in.

Above and opposite: **The Greystone Hotel, Hohauser's 1939 Nautical Moderne masterpiece, seen with two different color schemes in the 1990s.**

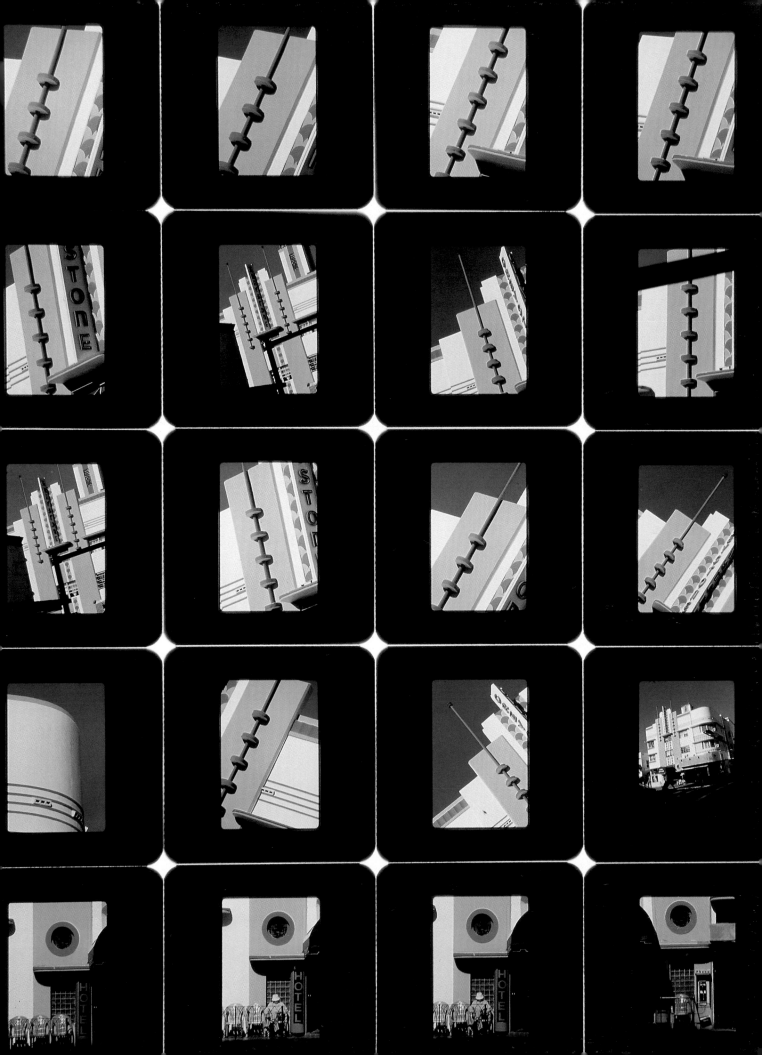

Opposite: **Nautical Moderne on the beach at Tenth Street.** *Above, from left:* **Decorative floral panel in bronze on the 1929 Chanin Building on Forty-second Street in New York City; the same motif in Tropical Deco on the 1936 Lincoln Theater in South Beach; and again on the lavishly decorated 1936 Helen Mar Apartments, a rare medium-rise Deco apartment house in South Beach that echoes its taller cousins in Manhattan.** *Below:* **Deco-detailed rooflines of South Beach.** *From left:* **The Webster Hotel (1936) by Hohauser; the Adams Hotel (1938) and the Marlin (1939), both by Dixon.**

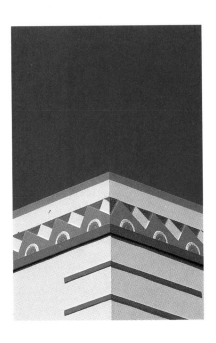

THE NIGHT SHIFT

"There are two shifts in South Beach. There's nine to five. And then there's nine to five." — South Beach neoprimitive painter Stewart Stewart

She's beautiful — achingly thin — and very sexy. She claims she's "a Martian," but she's really part Portuguese, Spanish, Cuban, and Italian. She won't say where she was born, but she was raised in New York City and Latin America. Her name is Yajaira.

That's pronounced "Jha-High-Ra," and she's one of South Beach's most sacred night creatures, a club goddess, likely to be found in the wee hours in a slinky gown and outrageously colored hair standing at the door of some chic nightclub — perhaps Glam Slam, the decadent dance club owned by the rock god formerly known as Prince, or maybe at one of her own crazy dance nights, which she throws at various little clubs she rents — holding a clipboard and choosing who to let in.

There may be a swarm of purring Ferraris, Lamborghinis, and Rolls Royces disgorging wealthy partygoers; there may be hordes of rowdy high-school kids with hickeys; there may be All-American football stars, rock legends, big drug dealers, tourists, movie studio heads, gangster girls with knives, famous novelists on book promotion tours, beautiful women, rappers, local drag queens, soap opera stars, suburban doctors and their wives, dangerously doped up Miami gangbangers, famous fashion designers, teenage Arab zillionaires, various South Beach friends and neighbors — probably all of the above

Opposite: **Yajaira.** *Right:* **Crowd clamoring to get into Glam Slam on opening night.**

and just about everyone else you can think of — and they're all crowding up to the velvet rope where Yajaira and the club's bouncers stand, waiting for her to decide who to let in.

"Working the door teaches you a lot about human nature," whispers Yajaira. As one of South Beach's most respected doorpersons (she has controlled the door of such legendary hot spots as Club Nu, The Spot, and Glam Slam), Yajaira has just about seen it all.

Sometimes, especially early in the evening, around midnight, some clubs will refuse to let almost anyone in, allowing a huge, anxious crowd to build up outside. The club may be totally empty inside, but the doorpeople and the beefy security guards beside them won't let a soul in. Not getting in drives the crowd crazy. But however artificially created this mob scene is, "When people pass by and see a big crowd at the door, it makes them want to go in," says Yajaira. "People will pay you anything to get in." Some supplicants will pretend to know the door-person and will greet him or her effusively, tipping them with a golden handshake, containing maybe a twenty, or maybe even a hundred or two, just to gain

admission to the club, or better yet to get access to one of the club's status-symbol inner sanctums, the VIP sections, where celebrities sometimes hang out. And because it's considered cool to be on the "comp" list and not to have to pay anything for admission, some people will surreptitiously pay the doorperson a big bribe just so they'll be waved right in and won't suffer the indignity of having to be seen waiting on line for a ticket as if they were some ordinary person, though, of course, lining up for a regular ticket would have cost them far less cash. Drug dealers and yuppies, says Yajaira, are especially likely to try to buy their way in.

Some other people, including many hip but not rich South Beach residents known to the doorpeople, get in right away for free, no problem. Breeze right in.

The key that unlocks the door is "aura," says Yajaira.

"People who are elegant or very androgynous, definitely they'll get in," she declares, adding without a hint of pretension, "I'm there for people to view me." Being the front person, embodying an elegant

aura yourself, working the door, choosing the right blend of people to let in, and making (and keeping) a club hot is a delicate art form, requiring the skills of a seasoned diplomat, fashion stylist, and zen priestess.

Imagining that they know the formula, many clubs try to synthesize excitement by creating artificial scarcity at the door, refusing to admit people even when the club is empty, and putting a glamorous woman (or drag queen) at the door. Yet plenty of clubs flop big-time, opening grandly and shutting ignominiously, sometimes after only a few days. Many an entrepreneur has lost a bundle in South Beach. The ambience inside a club is also of key importance for its success: the decor, the niceness of the staff, the choice of music…and most important of

Above: **Relaxing around 2:00 A.M. on a Wednesday at Bash, a club co-owned by actor Sean Penn.**
Opposite: **Door diva and drag queen Kitty Meow dances at Glam Slam, flanked by two club girls.**
Overleaf: **Just another weekday night at a club called Amnesia.**

all, the aura, hipness, and appearance of the people who come there.

Some clubs are a bit snooty, and getting in can be tricky, but plain, old-fashioned niceness counts, at least with Yajaira. "If they just give me eye contact and…if they're courteous to me," that helps, she says. Money isn't everything.

But if a club's a hit, serious money can be made. Yajaira tells of one well-mannered, hardworking club promoter in his mid-twenties taking home $5,000 or $10,000 a night while his club was (for a season) hot. And when a club's hot, even doorpeople can make big bucks. At Club Nu's peak in the 1980s, one doorperson there made about $75,000 in tips, says Yajaira, adding, "But the guy was good. All his clients paid to cut the line [i.e., get in without waiting], and his crowd was classy cocaine dealers. He made good money and he was only twenty-one."

Some doorpeople steal from the clubs they work for. (Scamming is rampant in South Beach.) One source tells of a major dance club where 2,000 people were admitted on an average weekend night, but, strangely, only about 900 official admission tickets were sold. At least one of the doorpeople was pocketing $4,000 to $5,000 a night for letting people in without tickets, plus he was reportedly dealing cocaine on the side. He was found out by management when he resold a complimentary ticket to the wrong person. The club didn't press charges because management didn't want to admit publicly that it had been so stupid as to be cheated this way, but scandals of this stripe are not uncommon in the cutthroat little universe of South Beach's nightclub business. One small promoter also claims business was sabotaged when rival clubs sent bouncers to scratch the paint of expensive cars parked outside, while the off-duty cops that police insist the club promoters hire were nowhere to be found. Stink bombs have also been thrown into clubs. And in nasty clubland power struggles, some club owners have tipped off tax inspectors to investigate the owners' own partners.

Before South Beach got so famous, the club scene used to be more, well, clubby. Artists Stewart Stewart and his wife Dena, who paint beautiful murals together, remember when the club scene was essentially friends throwing parties in abandoned buildings they would break into or perhaps get the keys to. Every night the "club" was in a different location. Veterans report there was a one-for-all,

all-for-one spirit to the community back then.

Club Nu, opened in 1987 by a group including legendary nightlife mastermind Louis Canales, was one of the first clubs to have a fixed location. Club Nu's opening had an Egyptian theme, including forty-five costumed performers recreating tableaux from the Book of the Dead, and there were rumors of couples making love in Egyptian sarcophagi. The opening lasted three days and three nights, attracted a reported 1,200 guests, and initiated a spectacular era in clubland.

Yajaira exemplifies the club people then coming to South Beach. She had first flown in — from New York in October 1986 — simply to cut someone's hair. (She was a hairstylist and choreographer back then.) She immediately fell in love with the neighborhood, then still in picturesque ruins. "Like a lost city," Yajaira described it later. "I felt that it needed to be explored. It was the right people at the right time.

"Later, the wrong people with money took over, but the aura was much prettier at that time. People would smile when they would see you…There were

only two clubs here, Club Z and Club Nu, they were happening clubs. It was underground, more totally progressive, and spiritual," insists Yajaira. "The music was something you didn't hear on the radio." True, the fabulous club scene of the mid- to late-'80s was fueled by mountains of cocaine (and tons of coke money), says Yajaira, who now tries to keep all drugs out of her clubs. But she says at least the marijuana and powder cocaine of the '80s were less dangerous than the drugs being dealt to many club kids in the '90s: crack and Special K (not to be confused with the breakfast cereal, this is a nasty concoction of heroin, cocaine, and horse tranquilizer). By the middle of the decade, the Colombian cocaine cartel was also pushing highly addictive, high-purity heroin in trendy South Beach clubs, hooking many beautiful young models and at least one prominent club night promoter. (A club night promoter is a South Beach entrepreneur who organizes, styles, and advertises a specially themed night at a nightclub he or she rents.)

Many of the hippest people, however, go to the clubs not to buy or take drugs but rather to enjoy the dancing, the incredible people, the sense of in-group exclusivity, and especially the seeing and being seen — all of which can still be heady stuff, at least sometimes.

During the mid-1980s, girls as young as fourteen were getting into clubs, young beauties like Tigre, a Haitian-American hip-hop princess, singer, dancer, and club kitten, now in her mid-twenties. "My parents were very cool," she says, "they knew I wasn't going to do anything crazy." There were many artists and creative people in the clubs then; South Beach was still a deeply bohemian haunt, not as glitzy as today. But plenty of models, photographers, and hip celebrities were visiting, recalls Traci, another young veteran club kitten who began hanging in the clubs in the summer of 1985, when she was fifteen. It was great, she recalls, adding, "Where else could you sit next to Madonna or Johnny Depp?"

Beautiful teenagers still get into South Beach clubs today, though their fake IDs better be good, and it always helps to know the doorpeople.

Above: **Maria — computer programmer by day, club kitten by night.**

In the '80s the club scene was much more underground and punk, and people dressed outlandishly. "The more crazy you looked, the more people wanted to talk with you," giggles Tigre now, wrapped in a cocktail dress and sipping a martini at a soigné private club named Lua on Espanola Way, where cabaret singer Bambi, a blonde bombshell with major cleavage, warbles jazz standards.

Raunchier scenes abound. In 1994 a now-vanished but lava-hot dance club called Velvet proudly presented some simulated sex shows on stage. The show looked like a cross between a Janet Jackson dance video and a slurpy porno video: tattooed bodies in bondage gear, whips and masks, men and women chained to a whipping post, that sort of thing. And it's said that live sex shows, where people really do it on stage, are available now and then around the scene. Some club nights I've attended had the flavor of *La Dolce Vita* orgy to them, with intimate acts in the back room, but then again, that's not so different from a really good party anywhere. And dancing on tables is virtually de rigueur in South Beach clubs, bars, and (at least after the dinner hour) in many restaurants. Are we having a good time yet? Late one Sunday night (Sundays tend to be much more decadent than tourist-infested Saturdays) at a chic Italian-run restaurant called Bang, I photographed a voluptuous woman stripping out of her blouse and dancing topless (another charming local custom), while others in the room, including the Panamanian dictator's daughter, Sandra Noriega, watched avidly or danced too. It was all so South Beach: exhibitionistic, voyeuristic, celebrity-obsessed, slightly decadent, somewhat snobby, very photogenic, and a lot of fun. Other revelers danced on shaky tables, one table finally surrendering and collapsing under the very high-heeled feet of five fabulous, undulating models. Unfazed waiters simply shoved the broken table out of the way, and the ravishing and ravished crowd danced on.

The hardest partying generally starts around 3:00 A.M. and runs past dawn. When I showed up at 1:00 A.M. to photograph one of Yajaira's S&M theme parties, which ostensibly had begun at midnight, she asked me why I'd arrived so early. Many musicians, hustlers, drag queens, bartenders, waiters, and other restaurant and nightclub workers like to party after they get off work; they're the real late shift powering the after-hours scene, along with those who form a sort of sexual underground.

Most of the night people don't have normal jobs. In fact, if you're a day person with a steady nine-to-five job, making the night scene on a regular basis becomes too exhausting, even if you take "power naps." It's much easier if you're a trust fund kid, or an artist with no set hours, or maybe a beautiful model or an international airline flight attendant with crazy hours, long layovers, and multilingual skills. (Award yourself 1,000 bonus points if you're willing and able to take long cruises on older playboys' yachts.) But to really be part of the night, to truly merge with the scene, you must totally surrender to it, give up any "normal" day life, and live like a vampire essentially only at night. Unless you have the money to just hang out (and many do) or a sugar daddy (and many have), you must get some job in the night world, maybe working in a club — or better yet, if you have the creativity, organizational skill, and personality to pull it off, you can become a club night promoter and produce your own imaginatively themed soirées, like Richie Rich's Big Kahuna at Lucy's Surf Bar beginning at 11:00 P.M. on Thursdays, or Madame Woo's Forbidden City at the Kremlin on Lincoln Road.

Welcome to a neo-Warholian night world, where nearly everyone becomes a celebrity, however briefly. But beware: the sycophant count is high. And many regulars themselves insist the nightlife they lead is vapid and meaningless.

On the other hand, it can be fun.

Sometime in the 1980s, South Beach became a place where people came to reinvent themselves. Among the ringleaders of reinvention were gay people, who poured into South Beach and helped urban-homestead the neighborhood. More especially, it was the flamboyant drag queens who flounced out of their closet around 1990, becoming a sort of girl gang of community court jesters, holy fools in a liberated zone, whose wit and creativity epitomized a certain South Beach attitude of friendly non-conformity and satiric style, applauded by gays and straights alike.

Many local drag queens (whose hour of greatest glory was probably when Madonna invited them over to her Miami mansion to party, ordered them to jump in her pool, and then dived in with them) are men in their mid-twenties, many of them refugees from uncomprehending parents and hometowns, who now subsist two and three to an apartment in South Beach, living on fast food and free drinks, saving their money for ridiculously expensive — $600 — but to-die-for Vivienne Westwood platform shoes or elaborate outfits from secondhand shops like Merle's Closet, where, as the sign in the back says,

Lupe, ad-libs friendly insults, and hosts several popular South Beach drag shows under the longest lashes, heaviest makeup, and biggest wig this side of salsa singer Celia Cruz.

In a double-espresso-thick Cuban-American

EVERYTHING IS F-A-B-U-L-O-U-S, and the manager is none other than Yajaira.

Each queen is required by tradition to create her own unique persona, beginning with her drag name, for instance: Patti Kakes, Kitty Meow, Taffy, Sexcillia, Honey Sweet, and the foul-mouthed but funny Varla (a.k.a. Craig Coleman), with her squabbling House of Varla, her big Bitch of the Beach beauty contest at the Warsaw Ballroom (the talent competition was especially keen), and her very strict Summer Camp for Wayward Boys, also at the Warsaw. But the king of the queens is in my view Adora, a little mega-blond Latin bombshell, born Danilo De La Torre, who passionately lip-synchs bravura Latin ballads by such ultra-vamps as La

accent, Danilo explains: "Danilo is like a very seemple and normal person and nothing to do with glam-moor, nothing." Indeed, on the street you'd hardly notice Danilo, a short, well-dressed man. "Adora is someone I built up," says Danilo, "and she has to be, like, a lady. Has to be chic, has to be, like, you know, nice dresses, has to be, you know, glam-moor, but a funny glam-moor…Not like a real woman or anything like that. A glam-moor, but exaggerated…Everything is big: big hair, big eyelashes, big lips…big, big, big, big." Her wig is often beyond big: the word "humongous" comes to mind.

Are you ever hassled on the street? she was asked.

"Never, never, never. A little screaming in the street, like, 'Faggot!' or 'What the hell is that?' Tiffany once got beat up on the street and Kevin Aviance, but, please God, it never happened to me. Never, never, never…The people who scream on me bad things are really a minority. The rest of the people, if they're straight and they don't know how to act, they

wouldn't say things like the gay crowd, but they can go like, 'Oh-my-God! You look sooooo good!'

"I think [drag] is a big movement. I don't want to say it's in now, but it's almost that…South Beach drag is very different, not any silicone or anything like that. We are very friendly, no fighting!" But what about the very loud-mouthed Varla, whose bawdy, onstage insult humor made her sort of a drag queen equivalent of Don Rickles? "Varla's trashy," conceded Adora, adding emphatically, "Warsaw was a club where people could really be free to dance and party and do everything you

Opposite, above: **Adora;** *below:* **as her creator Danilo.** *Above, left:* **Robert;** *center:* **Robert in his Chanel Noway drag with dog;** *right:* **Madam Woo, a.k.a. Alan.**

wanted…Everybody, everybody went to Warsaw."

The Warsaw is worth going to: a cavernous, pansexual, Felliniesque disco spectacle on occasion, housed in a extraordinary Streamline Moderne building designed by Henry Hohauser as Hoffman's Cafeteria in 1939, on the corner of Collins and Espanola Way.

With fifteen or twenty

drag queens prancing around South Beach at night, some unusual encounters are bound to develop. Chanel Noway (whose real name is Robert) looks like Barbra Streisand when he's in drag. "I've had experiences you wouldn't believe," said Chanel. "I had this little pink top on with no fake boobs or anything and this guy, he grabbed me and said, 'You're coming home with me!' Then he grabbed my crotch — and asked, 'Are you a guy?????' He looked like an airplane crashed. I said, 'You've been grabbing me for a half-hour!' I think he was drunk… I think it was the way I kissed."

But you don't have to be a drag queen to come to South Beach and reinvent yourself. Other sorts of scenesters also create club names and personas for themselves. For example, there's back-alley club night promoter John Hood, who affects 1940s

gangster garb; artist Bobby Radical, whose look is, well, radical; and then there's Amir Amour, an articulate, twentysomething black former art college student who sported a platinum blond Afro plus a '70s disco wardrobe worthy of Funkadelic and attracted some of the most beautiful women on the Beach to his Sunday afternoon Motor-Booty roller-disco parties in Lummus Park, which he promoted under the name M.C. Love God. More than in most places, in South Beach life *is* theater; and the nightlife is a high comedy laced with burlesque moments and tragic undercurrents.

With its cast of thousands, including the drag queens, the models, the celebrities, the paparazzi, the press agents, the rich, the poor, the street people (like the guy named Gypsy Vagabond who lived in an alley, set up his easel around midnight on Espanola Way, and painted impressionistic cityscapes, sometimes while wearing a cape and a mask), plus the buildings, the trompe l'oeil–decorated restaurants, and the pulsating nightclubs as stage sets — the town is a spectacle at night.

The sheer beauty of so many people in South Beach is startling. No less an authority than *Playboy* reports that South Beach has "a greater concentration of female beauty…than has ever occurred in the history of the planet…We are talking about 120 blocks. According to Irene Marie of the Irene Marie Model Agency, 1,500 models live in these blocks year-round. The math is simple. There are about thirteen beauties per block."

This is no exaggeration, at least during the Season when most of the models are in town. There might be ten times more models in New York or Paris, but there they are scattered throughout a huge, cold city; while in South Beach in winter, literally hundreds of phenomenally fine-looking professional super-beauties from every corner of the world (plus countless young, eager, wannabe models) are concentrated in one sunny, warm, square-mile let's-party zone, where micro-bikinis with Rollerblades; tight cut-off jeans with the fly half-open; and tiny designer evening gowns and towering high heels on towering babes are the sort of eye-catching fashion statements you bump into every day, everywhere: on the street, on the beach, in the gym, in the supermarket. Meanwhile, hunky male models — some gay, some straight — are almost as common as the fabulous women. Incredibly, at one point around 1993 there were some twenty-two modeling agencies in town. There's since been a shakeout, but there are still well over a dozen, including the offices of uber-agencies like Ford and Elite, and strong South Beach operations like Irene Marie and Michelle Pommier.

South Beach's narcissistic and voyeuristic cult of beauty sometimes freaks out even the models, the more thoughtful of whom wonder whether the values of the business are healthy. You're valued chiefly for how you look (though sense of style also earns you points). Still, if you can keep your head screwed on straight, the money's great. Despite the oft repeated mantra that "modeling is hard work," which is to an extent true, it beats the hell out of waitressing, working the checkout counter at K-Mart, or keeping up

Previous spread: **The elegant Imperial Hotel, designed by Dixon in 1939, and renovated extensively by Tony Goldman in the 1990s.** *Above:* **Erotic dance performance at a club called Velvet.** *Opposite:* **Stefano's Italian deli, open in the wee hours.**

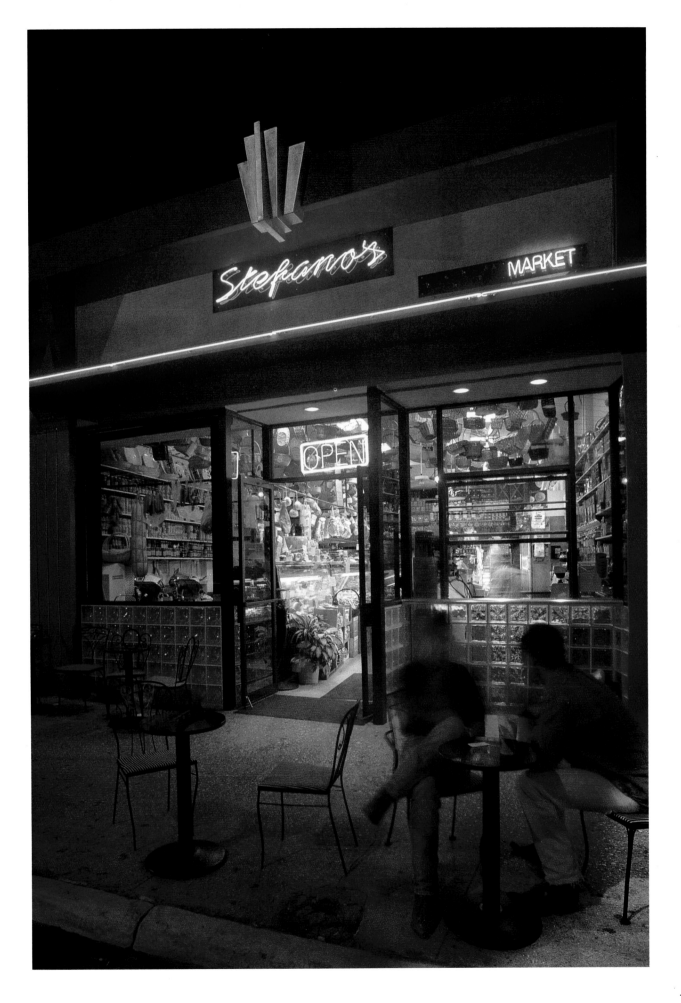

with the assembly line on the night shift at some margarine factory in New Jersey. The modeling lifestyle can be so fabulous that South Beach is besieged by teenage beauties and not-quite-beauties (both types arrive in droves, mothers optional) hoping to get started in the business. Sometimes they do, like Isamar Gonzales, a stunningly precocious, poised, and intelligent sixteen-year-old black girl from the Bronx, who was discovered by a modeling agency while she was on Rollerblades handing out nightclub fliers on Ocean Drive, a low-paying gig many girls do when they first come to South Beach. In less than a year the tall, slender, sexy, and sunny-dispositioned Isamar has been in Calvin Klein ads, Italian *Vogue*, *Mirabella*, and *Elle*. She looks well on her way.

But most girls don't make it. Even when they are signed to agencies, some models are rented out to decorate parties at clubs and achieve a lot less than superstardom, sometimes mere degradation. Be that as it may, the young beauties help delight and confound the carnival that's South Beach, not to mention drawing the Eurotrash playboys and other players who feed the nightlife. South Beach is super-visual, though some say superficial.

Underlying the throbbing nightlife, the permanent festival, with its wild straight, gay, and bisexual scene, is an epidemic, AIDS, which has turned the sweet victories of the Sexual Revolution into bitter ashes. South Beach's huge gay population is ravaged by AIDS, with obituaries appearing regularly, and it is well known to locals that some of the leading drag queens are dying. Varla wrote in her gossipy weekly newspaper column, "The Trick Report," about her AIDS and her admittedly self-destructive former lifestyle of super-promiscuous, often anonymous unsafe sex combined with heavy drug and alcohol abuse. (As death approached, Varla renamed her column "Safe," and it became more socially aware and poignant. She died in 1994.) But it is perhaps less recognized that many straight people are also being infected in the South Beach carnival.

"Very few people in South Beach are practicing safe sex, whether they're straight or gay," reports Randy Jansen of the Miami Beach HIV Center. "South Beach is a very young place…I'd say 70 percent of the people who are out partying are under thirty. There's high drug use, high alcohol use. This is a party town." He said many people believe in safer

sex "until the third drink." Another major cause of fatally unsafe behavior, he said, is "low self-esteem." And there's plenty of denial. Some local AIDS activists acknowledge there's a risky sort of *après-moi-le-déluge* disregard for the safety of others among some HIV-positives, lending a decadent Masque of the Red Death feeling to some of the compulsive partying.

One measure of a city's psychic (and economic) health is the quality of its newspapers. While mainstream newspapers are in decline throughout most of the United States, feisty alternative papers and glossy, gossipy magazines are thriving in South Beach; and the number of mainstream and alternative columnists writing about South Beach's torrid nightlife is staggering. The best ones are the delightfully upbeat Tara Solomon of the *Miami Herald* and the delightfully downbeat Tom Austin of the weekly *New Times*.

Austin describes South Beach as a sort of Dantesque high school from hell, only grown older and more corrupt but with the same adolescently fixated obsessions with status and looks within a tiny orbit of its own narrow glory. Typical of Austin's hypnotic weekly take on the scene:

> The gulag of Washington Avenue, a steamy incarnation of Kafka's Prague, wayward youths using fake identification cards and black-market drink bracelets as passports to early dissipation…A series

of acclaimed novelists — all swearing to the clean habits of the bourgeoisie and the artistic fervor of revolutionaries — coming to town and demanding sex, substance abuse and the American right to a vulgar weekend in Miami. Given this city's low-rent civic image, visiting luminaries might better be served if tax dollars went straight to the basics: complimentary convertibles, coke and amenable beauties.

And from another Austin column:

We're not taking any prisoners along on the national joy-ride...[South Beach] is a lawless landscape ruled by teen tycoons, easily mirroring Prohibition-era Chicago...a cornucopia of models and designer drugs replacing the era of bootleg liquor and flappers...Meantime, it's just say yes to alcohol, the club crawls with aging voyeurs...And so we all travel party to party, heedless and feverish, lost in the great engine of society, chasing the mirages of the night.

If Austin is the lyric and doomed F. Scott Fitzgerald of South Beach gossip columnists, overdosing on the pathos of publicity parties, Tara Solomon — herself a former South Beach door goddess, club night entrepreneur, and curvaceous magazine cover girl — is the irrepressibly innocent-hearted Candide of nightclub columnists, going everywhere and pronouncing it the best of all possible worlds.

"The party evolved from a quasi-civilized gathering to a festering volcano before our very eyes," she once wrote rather sweetly. One can only imagine what loving descriptions of degradation that same scene would have aroused in Austin.

Yet Tara can be Voltaire tart as well as Candide sweet. About Mickey's (a now-closed nightspot fronted by boxer, movie star, and Miami Beach High School graduate Mickey Rourke, who's something of a cult figure in France), Tara deftly observed:

"Without the name this would be nothing but a Bennigan's, complete with full restaurant service, pool tables, elegant decor, lots of boxing memorabilia, and a nice-size dance-floor. Slap Mickey's name on the marquee, and suddenly everyone wants to get in — even those who aren't French."

She once characterized her column as "party fluff and scandalabra." She labels supermodels "uber-

girls" and party-circuit regulars "celebutantes." She appears to live the party life she writes about, dressing with a sly, over-the-top glamour that often out-dazzles even the drag queens, and is rarely — if ever — seen in the same drop-dead outfit twice, be it a retro-'60s go-go get-up or a skintight, floor-length silver lamé evening gown. She insists her column is vapid, but don't let her fool you. Tara knows everyone and is one of the nicest *and* smartest people on the scene. She's a sophisticated and reliable guide, an astute observer, a witty writer, and — despite her glamour-girl persona — a hardworking newswoman, whose effortlessly champagnelike column is required reading for all those who'd venture into the night.

Columnists in café society — *Opposite:* **Tom Austin at work.** *Above:* **Tara Solomon and club night promoter Richie Rich at Starfish.**

THE NEIGHBORHOOD

"I claim that our city as a whole is an education."
— Thucydides, writing around 400 B.C. about Athens

We live in an odd era where people will drive three hours — or even three days — to go to a place like South Beach where they can get out and walk. The traditional urban experience of walking in an interesting and authentic neighborhood that's full of people has been largely lost in the automobile-centered universe of post–World War II American suburbia, where you need a car to get virtually anywhere and a person on foot is a fish out of water.

Nor has a richly stimulating, traditional urban experience been easy to find in the shell-shocked, crime-ridden, and poverty-stricken downtowns of too many of today's American cities, in decline partly due to the rise of the automobile-centered suburbs.

The enclosed shopping mall (surrounded by a sea of parking lots) is at once a response to and a contributing cause of the deterioration of both the big city's downtown and the small town's Main Street.

The malls' modern, corporate-managed versions of the agora (as the public marketplace was called in ancient Athens) seem to many people vaguely yet deeply unsatisfying — like the junk food the malls' food courts serve up. Nonetheless, in the absence of other pleasant pedestrian neighborhoods, America's

Above: **South Beach is a great town for walking.**
Opposite, left: **Classic Miami Beach: an older couple and a vintage screen door on a 1937 Hohauser apartment house. This graceful door was recently replaced by a graceless modern one (though the central portion of the old pressed metal work was saved and awkwardly attached to the new door).**
Opposite, right: **The flying saucerlike, Fifties Futura–style outdoor bar at the Clevelander Hotel on Ocean Drive attracts a young crowd.**

malls became magnets for many seeking human contact and community — particularly for seniors and teenagers (some of whom even call themselves mall rats). But who among us has not gone to a mall just to walk around and feel the energy of the crowd? Simply to feel the excitement of being in a public marketplace.

Made sterile by the lack of anyone living there (or even nearby), isolated by its vast parking lots, and constricted by its regulations, the standardized mall is, however, an ersatz agora, akin to the Disney version of Main Street that is the psychic centerpiece of Disney's land and Disney's world — stunningly

popular pedestrian environments, in which the car has been banished yet which are only reachable by car.

The success of such corporately idealized neighborhood substitutes is understandable. People need human interactions unavailable to them in their cars. But the modern mall and the nostalgic theme park strike many people as much too managed.

As calculated, formulaic, and well-executed as mass-market TV, the Great American Shopping Mall (like Uncle Walt's phony Main Street) can never

quite match the unpredictable excitement of an authentic shopping district in a real neighborhood like South Beach. For the mall seeks to privatize and regiment the public realm, the classical city's

traditional market- and meeting place — the original free market of both goods and ideas.

"Conservatives," as right-wingers insist on labeling themselves, seem to think that unfreedom (and all manner of other nasty social and economic consequences) comes only when governments control the private realm. But privatization of the public realm — the malling of the marketplace — has its problems, too. Privatization of the public realm has failed to preserve the old freedoms and sense of community (not to mention the historic architecture) of the traditional American neighborhood.

By contrast, the success of South Beach and other true neighborhoods is partly due to their keeping their public spaces public (especially that crucial sector, the agora, the marketplace, which provides the sensory-rich pedestrian, shopping, and meeting experiences that virtually all human animals, not least the sensory-deprived, mall-rat suburbanites, still crave.)

South Beach's main shopping and restaurant districts — Ocean Drive, Washington Avenue, and Lincoln Road — remain gloriously public spaces.

Ocean Drive is virtually an extension of one of America's most beautiful public beaches. Its liberal dress code, determined unofficially by public consensus — topless sunbathers welcome on the beach, bikinied Rollerbladers in Lummus Park, and shirtless bodybuilders at the sidewalk cafés — would cause sensory overload, not to mention a summoning of the security guards, at even the most sophisticated local Galleria Mall.

Washington Avenue, meanwhile, is a bustling commercial boulevard, a free market where almost any kind of business, be it a realtor selling only condos or a store selling only condoms, can vie equally for pedestrians' attention. At night, street artists spray-painting beautiful images on paper for only $15 or so coexist with boutiques offering clothing for thousands of dollars. Also on Washington Avenue, drag queens (Eeeeek! Someone call Mall Security! We don't want to offend the customers!) present one of their loudest and funniest shows: dancing queens loudly lip-synching songs (from Salt-n-Pepa to Marlene Dietrich) in a trellised outdoor restaurant — right next to Miami Beach Police Department headquarters, no problem.

As for Lincoln Road: Carl Fisher's great shopping boulevard is now a true open-air pedestrian mall with trees, fountains, and decorative structures (little Jetson-like pavilions and whimsical colonnades — what architects call follies — designed in 1959 by Morris Lapidus, Miami Beach's jet-age "architect of joy," as he's been dubbed, who also designed the landmark Fountainebleau Hotel, a couple miles to the north, in his fabulously sculptural Fifties Futura style.)

Venerable Lincoln Road's revival depends on artist's studios, galleries, one-of-kind restaurants, theaters, and sidewalk cafés: all unlike anything you'll ever find in a standardized corporate mall or Disneyworld. And people love it. They're once again coming from all over South Florida — indeed, from all over the world — to promenade and shop on Lincoln Road.

In ancient Athens, the Agora was an assembly point not just for the commercial life but also for the political and social life of the city. In fact, the Greek word "agora" came to mean an assembly place for the city, and from that evolved to also mean the city's "assembly," i.e., its political decision-making forum. The Roman Forum was actually modeled on the Greek agora. Centuries later, Lincoln Road, too, is something more than simply an open-air shopping center.

On Lincoln Road you'll also stumble upon typically nonconformist South Beach happenings, often reflecting the political and social developments of the day. It could be a gay kiss-in to protest a café's alleged homophobia; or a Cuban refugee raft, set like a floating sculpture upon a city fountain by some musicians who found the poignantly primitive, hand-built boat on a nearby beach where some new arrivals had abandoned it. Musicians, some hired by the cafés and others simply busking for tips, also perform in the streets. Meanwhile, chroma-crazed artists periodically dart out of nearby studios to give the Lapidus follies wild new paint jobs.

Lincoln Road is a truly public space with great freedom of assembly: artistic, social, and political freedom that should always be maintained, for it is the very spirit of the South Beach revival — in the tradition not just of the Athenian Agora but of the English commons and the Boston Commons, too.

The term "pedestrian neighborhood" doesn't quite convey the totality of the transportation picture. City officials and urban planners are slow to focus on it, but the people have voted with their bicycles: South Beach is a bicycle town. On a bicycle, you can get virtually anywhere in ten minutes or less.

Above: **Bike riding in Lummus Park.** *Opposite:* **Sitarist Stephan Mikés at the World Resources Café on Lincoln Road.**

Knobby-tired all-terrain bikes are especially cool for riding on the beach at sunset. (Bicycle theft is rampant, though, so lock your bike well when you go into a shop or restaurant. Parking meters and Art Deco metal railings make handy hitching posts on which the locals lock their steeds.)

Meanwhile, a flock of younger people, particularly models with great bodies, have taken to Rollerblades; and like a mutated new species of superheroic pedestrians they glide, effortlessly graceful, Mercury-swift young gods and goddesses with backpacks and 'blades — and very few clothes.

By contrast, getting around by car is slow and frustrating. Parking, particularly for big American cars, is difficult to find, especially at night around the busiest restaurant, shopping, and entertainment areas (making suburban-conditioned Americans go bonkers, convinced as they are that an on-site parking spot is their constitutional right and that walking a few blocks is unfair). So city officials, real estate developers, and backward-looking merchants obsess about parking. And admittedly, Rollerblades or bicycles are not options for everyone, especially those coming long distances or in rainy weather.

"But there never will be enough parking," warns noted town planner Andres Duany, "and any attempt to provide enough parking will destroy the city. It's stupid to destroy your city to provide parking [for people coming from outside]. The priority should be to the people who live here."

One solution could be to build parking in an outlying part of South Beach and bring back trolleys to carry visitors into the city center, where walking is the best way to get around. Or maybe a fleet of highly maneuverable motorcycle-based jitneys (six-to-ten-passenger, three-wheeled vehicles), like those used in New Delhi and other crowded Indian and Pakistani cities, would be better and cheaper than trolleys. South Beach artists could be hired to paint the vehicles, which would have cloth roofs and open-air windows. The idea would be to make them fun to ride.

One of South Beach's chief attractions is that it's a place where it's easier to walk than to drive a car. Making it much easier to drive in South Beach would inevitably also make it much harder to walk there — upsetting the pedestrian-friendly ambience that people love. But as late as 1994, some city officials showed they didn't understand the local dynamic when they proposed making Ocean Drive a one-way street to speed up car traffic. This horrified Don Meginley, a leader in the Ocean Drive Association, a savvy group of business owners. The last thing the street needed, said Meginley, was a faster-moving vehicular stream, making it harder for pedestrians to cross it. The street remained two-way, slow, and pedestrian-friendly: one of the planet's best places for civilized people-watching from its countless veranda restaurants and sidewalk cafés.

Ocean Drive, Washington Avenue, and Lincoln Road are the great boulevards that most visitors stick to, but most of the locals live in small Art Deco or Mediterranean Revival apartment houses nearby, on quiet streets just west of Washington, in a residential neighborhood of great charm and architectural beauty. Many of the houses were designed by Hohauser, Dixon, and the other Tropical Deco masters who did the great Ocean Drive hotels. Decorated and streamlined facades — including many extraordinary doorways — make every block of this residential area picturesque. There's a human scale to the little apartment houses and single-family homes. With all their fanciful decorative elements, these happy buildings seem to be almost greeting people. Strolling, biking, or 'blading in this residential neighborhood is a pleasure.

The town's pedestrian-friendly style and sense of community inspired the so-called New Urbanists — the intellectual ringleaders of what's also been called the neotraditional town planning movement. This design movement has attracted enormous international interest by breaking out of the postwar, automobile-oriented suburban mold that has proven so constricting.

The Miami-based husband-and-wife team of architects Andres Duany and Elizabeth Plater-Zyberk are the New Urbanists behind the internationally acclaimed and much-photographed neotraditional wood-frame town of Seaside in northern Florida. England's Prince Charles, a critic of much modern development, also hired Duany and Plater-Zyberk to design an upscale resort village, called Windsor, on 416 acres the prince owns in Florida's Indian River County. Duany and Plater-Zyberk were among the young architects and preservationists in Barbara

Opposite: **Parking problems and tickets are endemic; not even mermaids go free.**

Capitman's circle in the late 1970s. And South Beach was a formative influence on their now much acclaimed pedestrian-oriented approach.

"Pedestrian appeal is of paramount importance," Plater-Zyberk said in an interview for this book. "Seeing a place of mixed use, resort and residence — work, shopping, and residence — and how that attracted people from everywhere to it, whether they were the old folks, or Barbara Capitman, or the young people getting excited about it: I think that must have had a large impact on us."

She and her husband say that mixed use and a mixture of ages and income levels (as in South Beach) make for a vibrant, enjoyable neighborhood — the exact opposite, they say, of many contemporary suburban developments that effectively segregate people of different incomes and even different age levels. Uses are also strictly segregated by zoning in most of the postwar suburbs that many people find so dull and oppressive without quite understanding why.

For instance, offices can only be in office "parks," or in commercial strips along secondary highways, not in residential areas. And shopping must be in "centers," also removed from residential neighborhoods. Each residential subdivision is usually isolated from all other subdivisions. It's often impossible to walk directly from one to another. Each development, be it a shopping center, a residential subdivision, or even a school, is often reachable only by one entrance road. This entrance road may be a cul-de-sac, or a dead end. From the air, each such subdivision or office park appears almost isolated, self-contained in a separate pod, each pod connected only to the main feeder road and not linked directly to the others by a web of many little roads, as you would see in older neighborhoods. The results of pod planning: office areas are eerily deserted at night, while the residential districts are almost ghost towns by day. The clustered development of nearly identical housing units tends to concentrate people of one income level into small, homogeneous enclaves, which curiously lack any focal point such as a town square, post office, or main street where people traditionally meet. Meanwhile, it's hard to reach even a "convenience store" without having a car; and people without cars, such as children or the elderly, are curtailed in their movements. Many busy streets even lack sidewalks and are dangerous for pedestrians.

Furthermore, those residents who do have cars are often stuck in traffic jams on the ugly and overcrowded local highways onto which all the cul-de-sac, office park, subdivision, shopping center, and school pod roads dump them. And "rush hour" on this highway seems to last half the day.

On the other hand, consider South Beach: home/office/studio combinations are common; and apartments can be found above stores. Old and young, gay and straight, rich and not-rich, all live in the same fascinating neighborhood. Everything is in walking distance, including all sorts of interesting stores. Cars are inconvenient and are used sparingly by residents. Meanwhile, the streets and sidewalks are almost always picturesque and full of human interactions, particularly at the main gathering places like Lincoln Road, Ocean Drive, and neighboring Lummus Park.

Now, guess which place, suburbia U.S.A. or South Beach, is considered one of the world's most exciting neighborhoods in which to live?

The underlying reason South Beach appeals to people is not new: it is a traditional neighborhood, an urban village on the age-old model. Yet it was South Beach's beautiful and useful urban fabric that local developers and politicians like Abe Resnick tried to destroy, apparently not able to see the value of restoring it when it had become frayed and soiled. Even now, when the success of the renovated neighborhood is obvious, some developers and local politicians, hoping to cash in on the preservationists' success, have proposed such urban fabric-stretching projects as: out-of-scale, high-rise condos to loom over neighboring little Art Deco masterpieces; new mega-hotels (with or without gambling casinos) to be built in traditional, intimate low-rise neighborhoods; and a controversial shopping mall and condo complex designed by postmodern master Michael Graves for a key Ocean Drive site, which will involve gutting a historic Art Deco hotel, though part of its facade will be preserved.

All the breathless publicity about South Beach might make you think the neighborhood is populated entirely by supermodels and jet-setters. But believing their own press releases is what led some South Beach real estate developers, shop owners, and restaurateurs to lose their shirts. (When there are 135 restaurants in ten square blocks, not all can survive, not even in South Beach.) Yes, there are many supermodels who visit, plus some very rich people and plenty of yuppies, fashion people, celebrities, and poseurs. But the truth is most of the people who actually reside in South Beach are likely to be struggling artists or the hip young folks who work in the boutiques, art galleries, modeling agencies, photo labs, bars, clubs, hotels, and restaurants. As one resident put it with only some exaggeration: "This is a neighborhood of waiters."

Typical of many young people who live in South Beach is Kim Capron, a twenty-something photographer who makes ends meet by working at BWC Chrome Lab, the best professional photo lab on the Beach. "Any time an area gets really trendy and successful, the people that made it cool usually can't afford to live there anymore," she worries.

Like most Beach veterans, she says the club scene was more inventive a few years back, but feels the neighborhood still has an incredibly intimate and friendly sense of community, like a village, adding, "There's a certain kind of person who chooses to live here. It's generally someone who's not mediocre, not Middle American…The people here are bizarre. In my building alone there's a Haitian drum troupe and Johnny Dread and his [reggae] band. They all live there…I mean, the Haitian drum family is in one apartment: there's sixteen people. And then there's Michelle, she's the heavy metal waitress; and then there's Forest, he's a model…It's like a warped Melrose Place…They're really cool, and these people are not the kind who want to live in a prefabricated house in Kendall [a Miami suburb]. They want their dwelling to reflect some kind of style."

Fear that gentrification and overdevelopment will drive out the artists is widespread. Gentrification has already displaced most of the elderly whom Capitman had wanted to help. As late as 1992, there was a kind of balance between the old and the new on the streets of South Beach. Wizened Jewish retirees; poor Latino and Haitian immigrants; young fashion-punk-artist club kids with crazy hair; and international, fashion-forward model-types all rubbed shoulders in a funky mix. But only two years later, most of the old people had vanished, and poor Hispanic households (many headed by women) were on the run. Feeling priced out and culturally adrift, many of the elderly had migrated north to new golden-age ghettos in Broward County, housing officials reported.

Soaring rents and real estate taxes have also pushed some artists out. Too often their studios have been replaced by unoriginal stores selling overpriced jeans. The smartest redevelopers such as Tony Goldman, Chris Blackwell, and the Robins family acknowledge that without artists South Beach would lose its hip, avant-garde cachet. The Robinses' company subsidizes some artists by providing fairly affordable studio space, notably on Espanola Way, and the nonprofit South Florida Arts Center, which wisely bought several buildings on Lincoln Road, keeps a strong artistic presence there with its dozens of studio and gallery spaces. Nonetheless, rents keep escalating, and many artists feel threatened.

City Hall insists it wants to promote South Beach's hip new identity as an international arts center, but the city's top officials can't seem to recognize good art — or good promotion — even if they bump into it on the street, which is exactly what has happened. With disastrous results.

In 1992 a spectacular crop of poster art blossomed on the streets of South Beach. Every week, almost every day, colorful new posters appeared advertising crazy-themed club nights, dances, or cabaret appearances in local clubs. Some of the posters were by a world-renowned artist, Kenny Scharf, who had recently moved to Miami, but most were by locally well known South Beach artists such as Lazaro Amaral, Kevin Arrow, and Jef Hernandez. The poster craze became sort of a community competition, with young club night promoters vying to produce the best and most inventive posters, meeting at Kinko's copy center at 5:00 A.M. to run off the newest ones. It reminded me of the throbbing excitement of San Francisco in the psychedelic '60s, when a new school of artists exploded onto the graphic arts scene with eye-grabbing posters advertising a cultural revolution in general, and more specifically the appearances of renegade rock prophets such as Jimi Hendrix and the Grateful Dead at the hippie movement's tribal dance halls, the Avalon and Fillmore ballrooms, in an urban village called Haight-Ashbury. Many of those beautiful posters are now in the art history books and are highly collectible.

South Beach's blossoming poster movement also called to mind the origins of the modern poster: Paris in the 1890s, when artists like Henri de Toulouse-Lautrec made posters advertising dance halls such as

the Moulin Rouge, which was a popular if somewhat disreputable haunt of famous singers, dancers, artists, dissolute aristocrats, prostitutes, drug dealers, and other demimonde types — not so different from the demographics of your basic South Beach dance club today. Toulouse-Lautrec's posters portraying some of the Moulin Rouge's denizens are also in the art history books now, recognized as world masterpieces.

Impressed by the quality of the new South Beach posters, I started photographing them on the street to document the movement. In a matter of weeks, I photographed nearly eighty different posters. I also became a South Beach poster artist when dancer Antolino Alvarez commissioned me to photograph his company, the Dance Express of Miami, and some of my photos were made into black-and-white posters — designed by Tom Korba of South Beach Grafix, my design associate on this book — to advertise the dance company's performances. I liked the way the nightclub posters would layer upon each other, new ones partly covering the rain-ravaged and sunfaded posters from earlier weeks. Walking along Washington Avenue and glancing at the posters became a good way to learn what was happening in the clubs that week.

The colorful posters were usually pasted onto drab concrete utility poles, boxy city garbage receptacles, and hulking gray metal boxes that contain traffic light mechanisms. Mostly, the posters advertised sexy nightspots, but some seemed to advertise nothing more than grand hippie themes, and bore purely noncommercial slogans like LOVE IS IMPORTANT, or VOTE MONEY GRUB. Call it art or call it satire, but City Hall was not amused.

The City Commission unanimously passed a law against posters. The law states that putting posters on public property such as utility poles "threatens the safety of pedestrians" by creating "visual clutter." City Manager Roger Carlton also declared posters to be "detrimental to our existence as a tourist mecca," despite protestations from club managers that tourists, especially Europeans, loved the posters and found them a good guide to the nightlife.

I interviewed Mayor Seymour Gelber about the controversy. He said he had voted against the posters without having seen any of them, but he nonetheless called them "an eyesore…advertising a product just like a billboard."

But Toulouse-Lautrec's posters were advertising, too.

"I'm opposed to any kind of sign, including those of Toulouse-Lautrec, on our utility poles," replied the mayor, adding, "This is not some contest between art and bureaucracy…I'm not against posters. My house is full of posters from museums."

Coincidentally, there's a fascinating new museum on Washington Avenue, the Wolfsonian Foundation, that collects "the decorative and propaganda arts," including posters. So I went to the Wolfsonian, housed in a lavishly renovated Art Deco building, and asked museum director Peggy Loar what she thought of the contemporary poster controversy. It turned out she was unaware of the posters in the street right outside her museum. But when I showed her dozens of photos of the banned posters, she said the posters were good and asked where she could buy some.

A stiff schedule of fines has succeeded, however, in almost totally ending the South Beach poster movement. New posters are rare now, although some of the original artists, nightclub promoters, and a few people who took posters from the street at the time have collections.

In a city like South Beach, aesthetic controversies abound. One fight is about what colors are proper for an Art Deco building. Originally, most of the buildings were painted white. After Leonard Horowitz's pastel Deco Revival palette became a hit, the city actually issued a regulation requiring owners to choose color schemes from a palette of seventy colors selected by Horowitz — a regulation widely ignored and little enforced. Some spectacular renovations by Dacra Development, including those of the Netherland, Leslie, and Carlyle hotels on Ocean

Previous spread and above: **Banned in South Beach — city officials claimed posters like these threatened pedestrian safety.** *Opposite:* **The Netherland.**

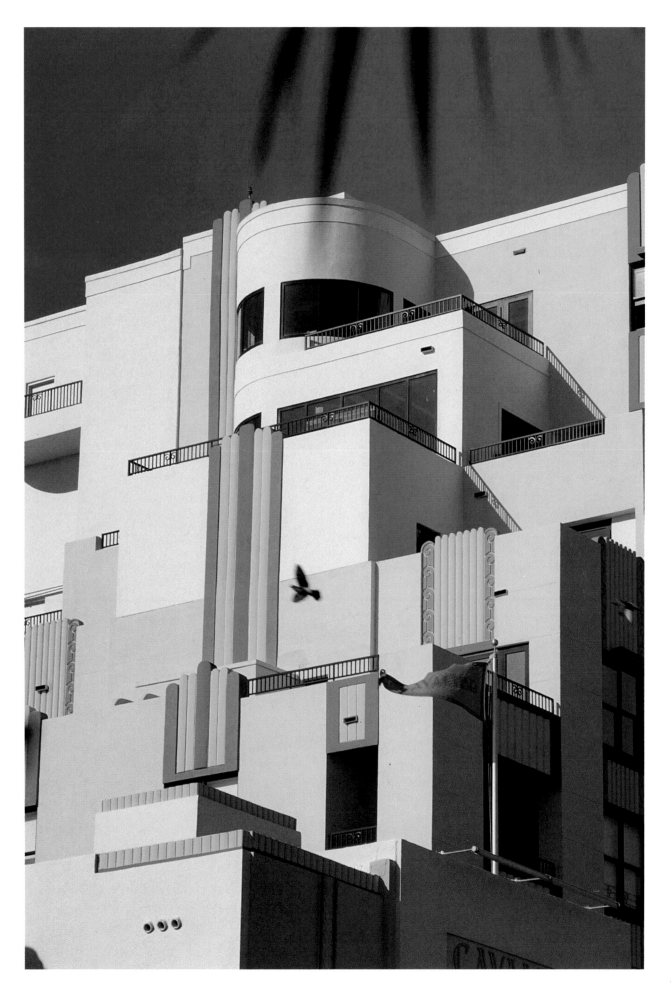

Drive have featured deep, vibrant, and bright colors chosen by London-based designer Barbara Hulanicki, who publicly declared pastels dead, triggering a taste war. Preservation League purists denounced the bright heresy and called for a return to Horowitz. Meanwhile, some survivors of the 1930s, including architect L. Murray Dixon's son, said the buildings shouldn't be either pastel *or* bright colors, but should instead be painted white, as their original architects had intended. Later, City Hall said it would draw up a new, approved palette, but the issue has never really been resolved. But, as Don Meginley of the Ocean Drive Association points out, paint jobs are not permanent.

More lasting are additions some developers are constructing on top of Art Deco buildings. Dacra, for instance, added three new stories, including a penthouse, atop the Netherland, a 1935 Ocean Drive hotel that Dacra renovated into a chic combination retail, office, and residential building. Absolutists such as architectural historian and planning professor Aristides Millas of the University of Miami denounced the addition, but others applauded it, and the redesign of the building won an award from the American Institute of Architects. People of goodwill agree that a certain amount of change to buildings in the historic district is necessary for their creative reuse, but exactly how much change is permissible is hotly debated. Particularly controversial are the questions of whether new, highly visible (but perhaps highly profitable) additions should be placed atop the buildings, and exactly how much of the buildings' historic interiors can scrapped.

Even more controversial is the continuing destruction of Art Deco buildings, most notably the Revere Hotel, built in 1950. In 1993 Italian fashion designer Gianni Versace bought the Revere for $3.7 million, then demolished it to make room for a swimming pool, garage, garden, and other additions to the building next door, a ramshackle 1930 Mediterranean Revival–style landmark that Versace was converting into his Miami residence. The Revere brouhaha split the South Beach community. On the one hand, everybody admired Versace as an artist. And here was an international superstar, a fashion genius who wanted to live in South Beach! Plus he was a major employer of top models, making him a very welcome neighbor to some modeling agency owners. Moreover, his expansion plans were beautiful. Versace's attorneys also argued that renovating and enhancing his 1930 Mediterranean Revival palazzo was far more historically valuable than preserving the 1950 Revere.

When Abe Resnick tried to knock down Art Deco buildings, he would often claim that the building in question was not a very good example of the style and therefore could be harmlessly sacrificed. Versace's people now were saying the same thing about the Revere. Of course, aesthetic rankings are subjective. But a good case can be made that the Revere was a handsome — and irreplaceable — example of late Deco, when Tropical Deco was disappearing into a more rectilinear International Style. And the preservationists argued just that.

More importantly, they argued that knocking down Deco buildings in South Beach is like pulling out threads from a fabric: pull enough of them out, and the entire fabric will fall apart. They said part of what makes South Beach great is not simply individual buildings but the synergy of so many period buildings in one neighborhood, forming a rare and priceless urban fabric. Keep destroying Art Deco buildings, and pretty soon you won't have an Art Deco district, just a handful of preserved buildings lost in a sea of new construction. And, said the preservationists, everyone who wants to demolish a Deco building will argue that his particular one is not artistically significant.

City officials replied that their hands were tied, that they couldn't protect the Revere because the building was not legally classified as "historic" (a designation the city claimed could be applied only to pre-1950 structures). Therefore the Revere could be destroyed. The Preservation League sued the city. Meanwhile the League's chairman, who favored Versace, resigned.

"The whole thing was *so* South Beach," wrote one local magazine. "A famous designer, a wrecking ball, lots of juicy press, a lawsuit, the usual accusations of betrayal and skullduggery." In the end the League withdrew its suit in exchange for promises that the city would close the post-1950 loophole in the law. The Revere was demolished, and Versace built his handsome, gorgeously landscaped, and

Opposite: **Mural at Tattoos by Lou on Fourteenth Street.** *Overleaf:* **Assistant Joanne Trangle touches up mural by Bill Wrigley at Wet Willie's, an Ocean Drive watering hole.**

119

well-protected swimming pool.

The internationally acclaimed renaissance of the historic district in South Beach, for which the preservationists worked so hard, has meant hundreds of millions of dollars to South Florida from improved tourism, higher real estate values, and an enormously enhanced business climate. In fact, Art Deco saved South Beach. Moreover, it has been great for the image and the business of the entire Miami area. The Deco Revival's success is also inspiring attempts to revitalize other parts of Dade County, including the middle and northern parts of Miami Beach, plus downtown Miami and Miami's so-called Design District, perennially touted as "the next South Beach," though it's actually quite different. In any event, South Beach's success raises many new questions:

Should Art Deco buildings outside Miami Beach's officially defined historic district be legally protected?

And what about South Florida's 1950s buildings, many of them post-Deco? Some are *very* '50s, embodying a totally different era in American culture and design. Could they be profitably renovated? They are just as old now (and almost as unappreciated) as the Deco buildings were when Barbara Capitman and the others first moved to save them.

In the 1990s developers with deep pockets began moving into South Pointe (the formerly deeply blighted part of South Beach south of Fifth Street) with new plans for high-rise projects. One was to be forty-four stories tall, which would make it taller than any other building in the Miami metropolitan area save a few (such as the First Union Financial Center office tower in downtown Miami), and there was talk of building other condo towers in South Pointe of sixty-five stories, eighty stories, or even a skyscraping one hundred stories. By comparison, New York City's Empire State Building is 102 stories. Many South Pointe residents feared such projects would be grossly out of scale and destructive to the intimacy of their urban village neighborhood. But as part of a compromise that Capitman struck years ago when she got her historic district, a much more pro-big-development set of zoning rules applied in South Pointe, and it seems inevitable that at least some new high-rises, as well as some more intimately scaled projects, will be built. A number of fine low-rise Art Deco and Mediterranean Revival buildings were destroyed by developers to make room for the new projects; but a number of other old buildings have been handsomely renovated. Some people argue that more high-rises in South Pointe will only make the low-rise buildings in the historic district more valuable. And compared to the Concrete Canyon, a much less monolithic, more postmodern design sensibility is evident in the plans for some of the controversial new towers.

And what about the Miami Design Preservation League, Capitman's old group? Some critics say the league is interfering too much with development now, while others say it isn't protesting it enough, especially in South Pointe. Almost everyone agrees the group does fine work throughout the year with its walking and bicycle tours of the district and its great Art Deco Weekend festival every January. But no one in the leadership, no matter how dedicated, has been able to completely fill Capitman's shoes.

Meanwhile, many of the hipsters who have lived in South Beach for years now miss the funkier, more intimate, and less commercial ambience the neighborhood had during its struggling days. As columnist Tom Austin puts it, "It's over. It's all about money now." But then again, Austin is famously gloomy.

Finally, there's the fight over gambling. In 1994, voters overwhelmingly defeated a state constitutional amendment that would have legalized gambling casinos — and would have allowed a giant casino to

Opposite: **The Don-Bar, 1937, by Albert Anis, one of hundreds of delightfully renovated small apartment houses in the district.** *Overleaf:* **The Publix supermarket chain built more than sixty such supermarkets in Florida from the late 1940s to the late 1960s. This one, known as Number 91, was built in 1963, with Charles Johnson as architect of record, but the basic design was actually sketched out by Publix Supermarket founder George Jenkins in the late 1940s. As a symbol of postwar American affluence and optimism, this building stands tall as a classic example of popular roadside architecture in the automobile age. The winged central pylon is reminiscent of the rocketlike tail fins that adorned cars of the period. The pylon is ringed by a cascade of neon tubing that Publix officials call "The Waterfall." This building does not yet have historic designation or protection.**

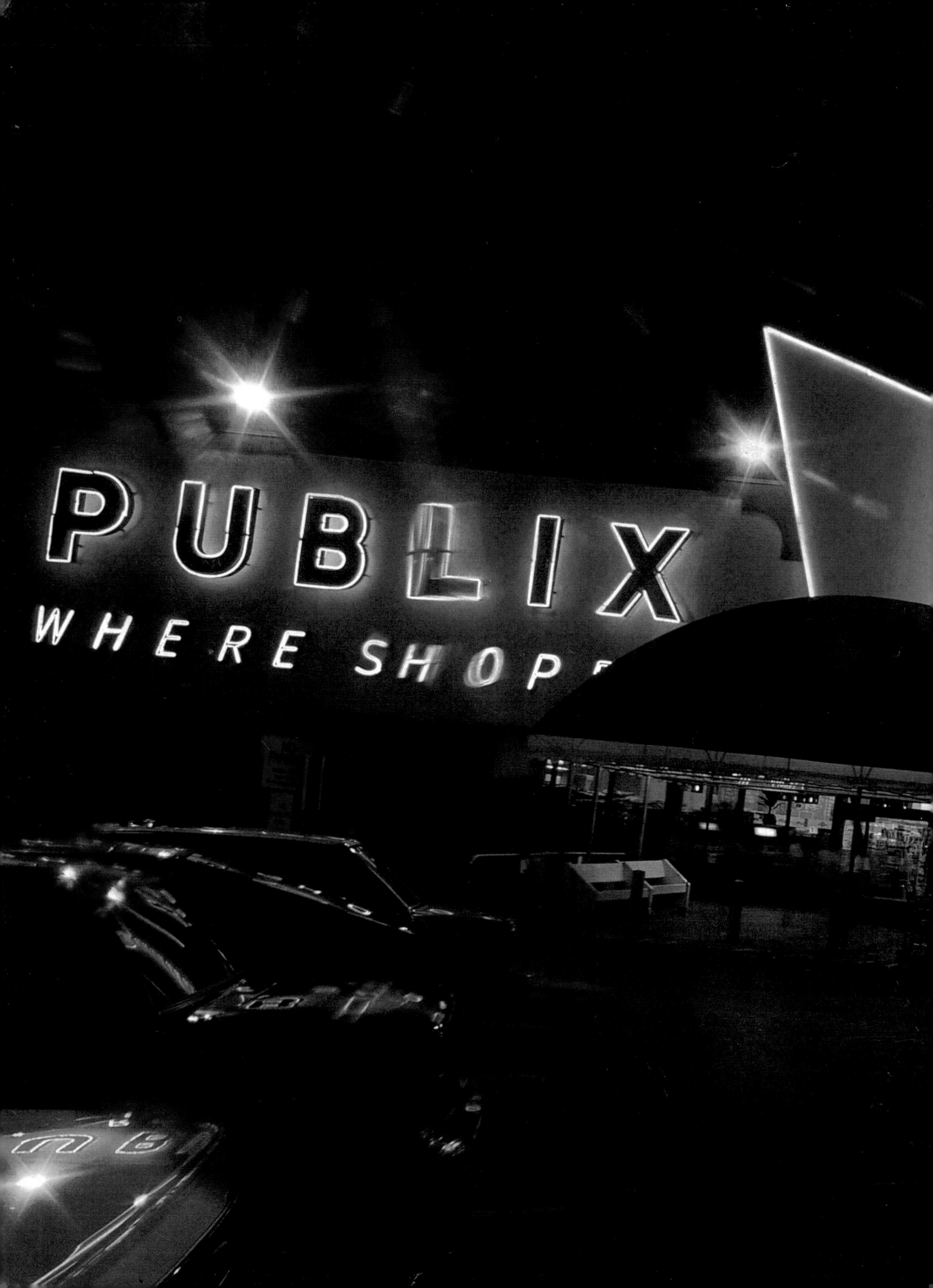
PUBLIX

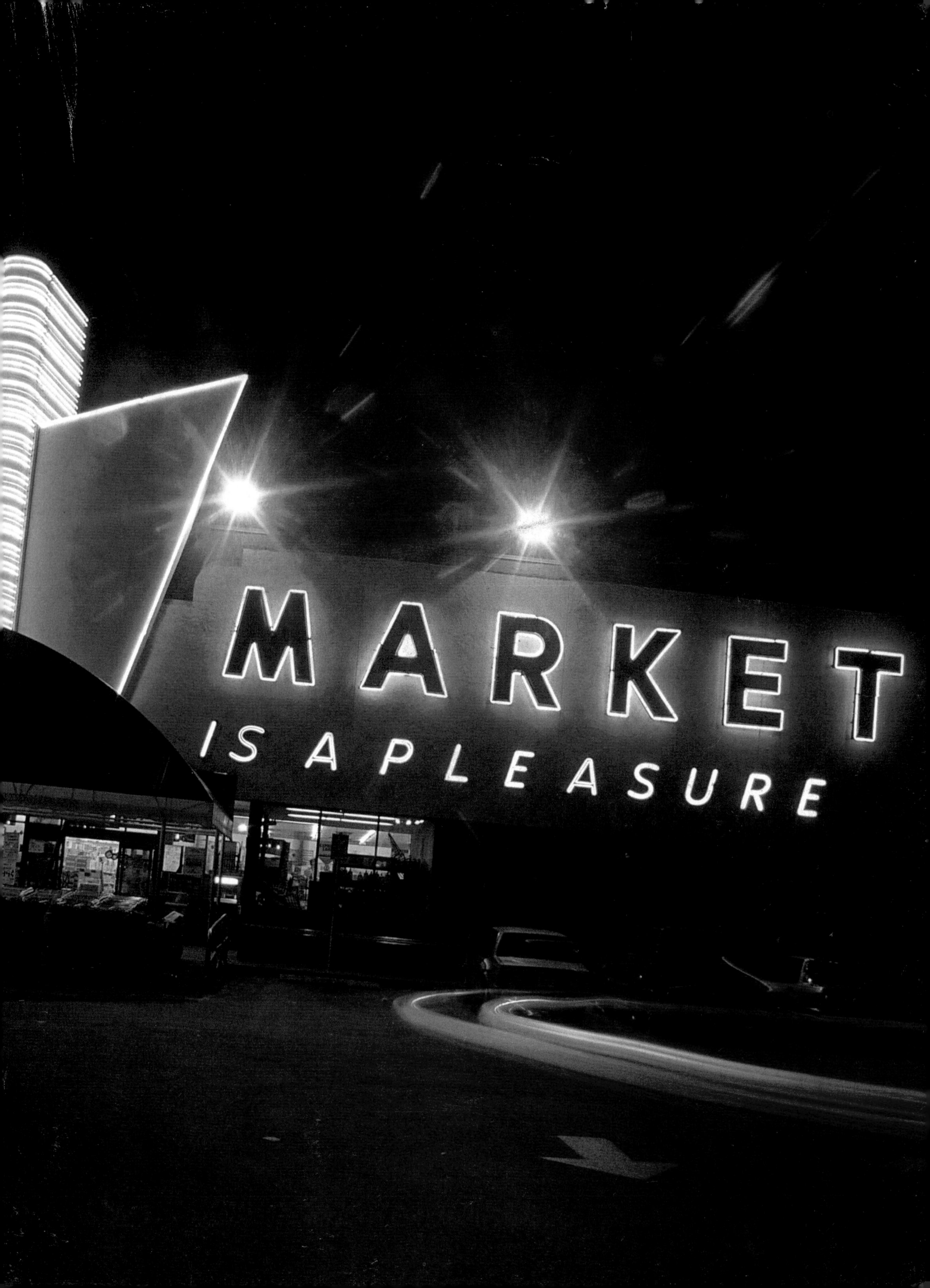
MARKET
IS A PLEASURE

be built in South Beach. Despite the vote, gambling interests vowed to keep trying to get casino gambling legalized — and into South Beach. Opponents replied that South Beach already had glamour, style, and prosperity and didn't need organized gambling, nor the down-market package bus tours a big casino-hotel might bring. But fights over gambling aren't new in Florida.

The first casinos were built by Flagler himself along with the state's first railroads. Though it was illegal, Flagler always built a casino (for wealthy tourists only, Florida natives not allowed) just next to — but not actually in — his grand Florida hotels. Soon the Florida gentry built grassy racetracks and little gambling joints in the woods. With Prohibition came the mob. First, there was Scarface Al Capone (who as part of his charm offensive in Florida was effusively entertaining the local press and much of the Miami establishment at his Palm Island estate, just off South Beach, on St. Valentine's Day 1929, while his gunmen in Chicago lined up some of Big Al's rivals in a garage and massacred them).

Later came hoodlums like Little Augie Carfano, Lucky Luciano, Frank Costello, and — most important of all — the mob's Jewish intellectual, Meyer Lansky.

In his later years, Meyer could be found devouring history and philosophy at the Miami Beach Public Library. Then he'd put on his dark glasses and walk across the street to Wolfie's delicatessen for coffee and cake, looking for all the world like a retired accountant. But until the day he died (of lung cancer) in 1983, Lansky was under constant FBI surveillance, for he was the brilliant mastermind of the mob's gambling operation not just in Miami, but

in Havana. In fact, Meyer organized crime in America; he was the organizer of organized crime.

This was before Vegas as we know it. Back in the '30s, '40s, and '50s, Meyer and the mob made Miami Beach into what was then America's greatest, albeit illegal, gambling resort. There were elegant gambling clubs and nightspots (one, the Latin Quarter, in a beautiful Deco building, was run by Lou Walters, TV interviewer Barbara Walters's father). The bookies were based in every hotel barbershop and usually in a cabana by the hotel swimming pool, too. An army of police chiefs and politicians were on the take.

From the first, Fisher hated the gangsters coming into his Miami Beach (or at least that's what he said), but he didn't, or couldn't, stop the wealthy gangsters from taking over much of the city. After Fisher sold his and Jane's beloved beachfront mansion, the Shadows, it became the Beach & Tennis Club, where, it is said, no one ever swam or played tennis. Fisher's former home was now a gambling casino.

The barely hidden gambling helped fuel a terrific nightlife. Miami was never the turf of any one family but was an "open city" where rival mob families gathered for business meetings and winter vacations. One Mafia daughter I interviewed described the late 1940s and early 1950s as glory years, with wives receiving brand new pink Cadillac convertibles every winter and snappily dressed gangsters squiring around showgirls who looked and dressed like Jayne Mansfield. Gamblers flew back and forth to Havana, and Miami Beach was called "the winter crime

Above: **Crew shooting a TV detective show in South Beach.**

capital of America," with casinos and whorehouses galore. Profits helped finance other mob ventures, including the heroin business.

But by the mid-1950s a nationally televised Senate investigation and crusading Miami newspapers had put a damper on Miami Beach gambling and the official corruption that made it possible. Also, the rise of legal gambling in the Caribbean and Las Vegas (which Meyer and his childhood friend Bugsy Siegel helped create) — plus faster airplanes to those places — made Miami obsolete as a big gambling resort. When Miami became inhospitable to casinos, Meyer, who split his Cuban profits with dictator Fulgencio Batista, simply remodeled the great old Hotel Nacional casino in Havana and reopened it in 1955, with Eartha Kitt headlining the floor show. He also ordered to be built a magnificent new twenty-one-story, 440-room hotel-casino in Havana to strengthen his already huge Cuban operations. Called the Riviera, it opened in December 1957. Only thirteen months later Castro took Havana, confiscated the hotels, and closed the casinos. It was truly the end of an era. But before it all ended in Miami and Havana, there was a now-legendary scene, with stars like Sinatra and his rat pack, Nat King Cole, Marlene Dietrich, Walter Winchell, Jayne Mansfield, Arthur Godfrey, Martha Raye, and Xavier Cugat hanging out, performing in, or even owning South Beach nightclubs.

The opening of the Fontainebleau Hotel in 1954 also figured in South Beach's decline. Erected on the site of the old Firestone Estate, a couple of miles north of South Beach, and designed in a superglitzy and colossal new style that expressed postwar America's new role as the most powerful (if not the most cultured) nation on earth, the huge Fontainebleau was the first of a series of giant hotels that moved Miami Beach's center of gravity north, away from South Beach.

The small Deco hotels in South Beach became passé. All the gangsters, high-rollers, and rich tourists now wanted to stay at the lavish new mid-Beach hotels. The new hotels all boasted nightclubs inside them, featuring top name stars. The "American plan," a package deal in which room rent at the new hotels also included meals in the hotels' own restaurants, also kept many guests from going out at night, badly hurting business at South Beach nightspots, restaurants, and hotels. This is when South Beach began filling up with retirees of modest means.

Now, of course, South Beach is back on top. Its new nightclub scene, mostly discos and some cabarets, is driven by the glamour of the modeling, film, and music industries; the underground party culture of the gays; and money flowing from all over, including from Latin and European investors and, it is said, from drug dealers looking to launder their cash.

As for political corruption, it's still around. In 1993 a Miami Beach mayor pleaded guilty to bribery, money laundering, obstruction of justice, and tax fraud in connection with taking payoffs from a prominent banker. The mayor, Alex Daoud, served only eighteen months of his five-year sentence, getting time off in exchange for testifying against two bankers. After his release in 1995 Daoud, who had been disbarred as a lawyer as a result of his felony conviction, said he was considering going to medical school on the island of Grenada and becoming a doctor.

Meanwhile, many South Beach business people think the Miami area in general — and South Beach in particular — should forget about trying to revive gambling, with all its potential crime and corruption problems, and instead should work to get a major movie studio or two built in the Miami area. In the 1990s, with Los Angeles becoming less livable due to a series of natural and social disasters, Hollywood had already been shooting more and more feature films in Florida, and some stars (notably Stallone and Madonna) have moved to Miami.

In any case, the key to South Beach's great revival and its worldwide popularity and fame as an art, fashion, media, and party capital has been its newfound status as a world architectural treasure; and many people are very bullish about its future.

"Everybody who comes to Miami wants to go to South Beach," smiles twenty-two-year-old Elizabeth Duey, a Miami native I found sunbathing on the sand there. "You can come to the Beach and have a great time, no matter what you do," she said, wiping her windblown hair from her face. "Just walking around and people-watching is great. I like what it's become…and it's only going to get better."

SPECIAL THANKS TO:

Bari Fletcher for telling me about South Beach * **Bill Kaufman** for launching me on this book * **Betty and Bob Nemeroff** for believing in the project and providing start-up money that made it possible * **Larry Wisser** and publishing contract attorney **Ken Swezey** of the New York firm Cowan Gold for excellent, patient, and enthusiastic counsel * **Pat MacFarlane** and the **Olympus Corporation** for keeping my cameras working and for the generous six-month loan of the superb Olympus Zuiko 24-mm shift lens I used to make many of the architectural photos, including the cover * **Bazhadar Vangelou, Robert Kindred, Eric Rose, Kim Capron, Brenda Schelley,** and **Lou George** of BWC Chrome Lab, the best color lab in South Beach, for fine E-6 processing * Ft. Lauderdale–based master printer **Norm Summey** for magnificent color prints * **Cliff Morrison, Steve, Mark Donehoo,** and **Peter Mansfield** of Hot Shots (on Washington Avenue) for beautiful color laser prints used in marketing the proposal * Sarasota architect **Terry Osborn** for introducing me to the urban planning ideas of **Andres Duany** and **Elizabeth Plater-Zyberk** that inform much of Chapter 6 * **Michael Kinerk, Dennis Wilhelm, George Neary, Betty Guiterrez,** and **Christine Giles** of the Miami Design Preservation League for all their help * The *Miami Herald'*s publisher, **David Lawrence Jr.,** and librarian, **Bill Whiting,** for permitting me to do historical research in their newspaper's invaluable archives * **Mary Ann Crenshaw** of the Italian fashion magazine *Amica* for many things, among them assigning me to photograph the Eleventh Street Diner * **Mark May,** creative director of *Gulfshore Life,* for his wonderful help in the early design work * The late **Howard Sochurek,** a great *Life* magazine photographer, for also being a great friend and mentor * **Bernard Gotfryd,** author and former *Newsweek* photographer, for his friendship and advice * Computer expert, layout artist, and friend **Tom Korba** of South Beach Grafix, my design associate on this book, for all his tremendous skill, sage advice, hard work, and good humor * My publishers, **Dick and Jeannette Seaver** of Arcade (and their associate **Cal Barksdale**), for believing in me, this project, and the proposition that maximum creative freedom produces the best results * **And to all the people who talked with or were photographed by me for this book.**